May You Have a Merry Christmas

# May You Have a Merry Christmas

*and the Best New Year Ever!*

## JOHN H. LEITH

RESOURCE *Publications* · Eugene, Oregon

MAY YOU HAVE A MERRY CHRISTMAS
and the Best New Year Ever!

Resource Publications
An Imprint of Wipf and Stock Publishers
199 W. 8th Ave., Suite 3
Eugene, OR 97401
www.wipfandstock.com

ISBN 13: 978-1-60899-423-6

Manufactured in the U.S.A.

*This Christmas greeting goes to friends whom I have known as students of theology and now as colleagues in the ministry.*

# Contents

# Foreword

D R. JOHN H. Leith (1919–2002) enjoyed Christmas. He appreciated it especially as a celebration of the goodness of this world that God not only created but also, in the incarnation of Jesus Christ, entered, blessed with his presence, and redeemed. And at Christmas he especially wanted to be in contact with, and to minister to, those whom he loved, those whom he had taught, and those whom he cherished as colleagues in the Christian and Reformed ministry of preaching, teaching, and pastoral care.

This little book comprises a collection of Leith's Christmas letters to his former ministerial students at Union Theological Seminary in Virginia. The letters grew lengthier and richer through the years. We have gathered them here so that others may enjoy reading them, also. The letters varied widely in typography, but no attempt has been made here to preserve the typefaces, to copy the Christmas stationery which he bought, or to convey the shape of paragraphs typed around the pictures. Instead, some effort has been made to standardize formatting, indentation, italicization, quotations, and so forth.

Moreover, in Leith's six earliest letters (1973–78), it has seemed helpful for the sake of formatting and understanding to provide one line introductions to identify the quotations as quotations. His occasional use of the abbreviation "UTS" has been expanded to "Union Theological

Seminary" for the sake of a wider readership. Where it has been needed and possible, additional bibliographical information has been given for references. Where it has seemed helpful to the sense of the letters, additional information has been provided in footnotes.

The Foundation for Reformed Theology is especially grateful to those who provided us copies of the various letters and inserts: Dr. David A. Dickerson, Dr. Daniel W. Massie, Dr. Allen C. McSween, Dr. William P. Wood, and the C. Benton Kline Jr. Special Collections and Archives of the John Bulow Campbell Library of Columbia Theological Seminary.

I have chosen as a title for this collection the exclamation with which, in one form or another, he completed most of these letters: May You Have a Merry Christmas and the Best New Year Ever!

James C. Goodloe IV, Executive Director
Foundation for Reformed Theology

# Christmas 1973

WILLIAM TEMPLE has this to say about the good news of
the revelation of God in the person of Jesus Christ:

> The Gospel is precisely the proclamation of the
> good news that God exists and is eternally what
> we see in Jesus Christ. . . . It is worth while to
> point to the importance of the fact that the rev-
> elation is given in a Person and not in a set of
> propositions—not even in a set of propositions
> about that Person. It is to Christ, not to the Creed,
> that the world should look for its salvation. The
> Creed is important because it points to the one
> hope of Redemption; but its importance is sec-
> ondary, for it is not itself the source of saving
> power. Remembrance of this will save us from
> the central medieval blunder of imposing the
> rule of theology on science or art, or *enforcing*
> a submission of conduct to religion. The unity
> we week must come from the all-pervasiveness
> of the influence and spirit of a Person. The mes-
> sage of the Gospel to individuals, to groups, to
> classes, to nations, to races, is "Let this mind be
> in you which was also in Christ Jesus," and the
> same message is given to economists, to scien-
> tists, to artists, to poets, to novelists, to journal-

ists. Moreover, it declares that this is possible just because Jesus Christ is not only a historic figure like Socrates or Caesar but is the manifestation of that universal and eternal Spirit in whom we live and move and have our being, and who is Himself the source of our existence and sustainer of our life.[1]

Aleksandr Solzhenitsyn writes this about the courage of resisting falsehood:

Simple is the ordinary courageous human being's act of not participating in the lie, of not supporting false actions. What his stand says is: "So be it that this takes place in the world, that it even reigns in the world—but let it not be with my complicity."[2]

Christmas is a time for human grace—for goodwill and for support of person by person. Therefore, I am glad to express my best wishes for you this Christmas.

Christmas is also, and first of all, the celebration of God's grace. Therefore, I am glad to hope that your life will be made merry by His grace and that your study of theology and your vocation of preaching, teaching, and pastoral care in the Reformed tradition will be made strong by His providence.

John H. Leith

1. Temple, *Religious Experience*, 102.
2. Solzhenitsyn, "Nobel Lecture," 526.

## 2

# Christmas 1974

THE SIMPLICITY, the inner integrity, of the joy of Christmas distinguishes it from more common joys, and this Christmas joy ought to be and is the common greeting between those of us who have shared in the common tasks of theology and churchmanship at Union Theological Seminary.

Consider Rembrandt's "Adoration of the Shepherds":

> Here now we see a quite ordinary shed. Father is sitting on a wheelbarrow, mother on the straw. Shepherds are arriving with their wives and children. One has brought his bagpipe along. A small boy is gazing at the newly born child with great interest. Could there be a more human, a more ordinary scene?
>
> And yet something extraordinary seems to be happening in this scene and giving it a deeper meaning. . . .
>
> A handful of men have grasped the certainty and the truth contained in this incredible message of a saviour "wrapped in swaddling-clothes and laid in a manger" . . . And his mother? She is not sitting on a throne, she does not dream of parading her child before spectators. Her gaze is

> lost in the distance. Her joy is overshadowed by the grief she foresees in the fate of her son.[1]

John Calvin wrote this, while commenting on 1 Corinthians 1:17, on the importance of simplicity:

> The gospel should be administered in simplicity . . . that in a plain and unpolished manner of address, the majesty of the truth might shine forth more conspicuously, and the simply efficacy of his Spirit, without external aids, might make its way into the hearts of men.[2]

And Reinhold Niebuhr sought to avoid artificiality in preaching:

> At any rate I swear that I will never aspire to be a preacher of pretty sermons. I'll keep them rough just to escape the temptation of degenerating into an elocutionist.[3]

When asked what he learned from his period of study (1974) in Edinburgh, a Union Theological Seminary graduate replied, "I have learned to live simply."

The blessings of Christmas joy and Christmas simplicity be yours personally and in your work.

John H. Leith

---

1. Visser 't Hooft, *Rembrandt and the Gospel*. See Christmas 1996 below.

2. Calvin, *Corinthians*, 1:76.

3. Reinhold Niebuhr, *Leaves*, 9.

# 3

# Christmas 1975

MARTIN LUTHER put it simply and plainly in his "Ninety-five Theses":

> The true treasure of the church is the most holy
> gospel of the glory and the grace of God.[1]

This greeting brings to you the very best wishes for a joyous Christmas and the happiest New Year ever. It also states the hope to colleagues in the theological task that this will be the best year ever for us in the theological service of God, especially in theological preaching, teaching, and pastoral care.

John H. Leith

---

1. Luther, "Ninety-five Theses," 31, thesis 62.

# 4

# Christmas 1976

KARL BARTH wrote this about the incarnation in "The Homecoming of the Son of Man":

> There are two elements in the event of the incarnation as it is attested in Jn. 1:14. If we put the accent on "flesh," we make it a statement about God. We say—and in itself this constitutes the whole of what is said—that without ceasing to be true God, in the full possession and exercise of His true deity, God went into the far country by becoming man in His second person or mode of being as the Son—the far country not only of human creatureliness but also of human corruption and perdition. But if we put the accent on "Word," we make it a statement about man. We say—and again this constitutes the whole of what is said—that without ceasing to be man, but assumed and accepted in his creatureliness and corruption by the Son of God, man—this one Son of Man—returned home to where He belonged, to His place as true man, to fellowship with God, to relationship with His fellows, to the ordering of His inward and outward existence, to the fulness of His time for which He was made,

to the presence and enjoyment of the salvation
for which He was destined.[1]

Christmas, when our faith is celebrated and renewed,
is a good time to renew fellowship, and for those of us who
have studied theology together to renew our common commitment to the integrity of the faith and to the integrity of
a personal and public life congruent with that faith. On this
commitment, on the clarity and integrity with which we
perceive the Christian message and its accompanying style
of life, the church depends humanly speaking, especially in
this time when the secularization of the church and its ministry has eroded its distinctive theology and its distinctive
moral commitments.

May this be a very joyful Christmas, and may this be
the best New Year ever.

John H. Leith

1. Barth, *Dogmatics*, IV.2, 20–21.

# 5

## Christmas 1977

CHRISTMAS IS a time of thanksgiving, about which John Baillie wrote this:

'The Lord Jesus the same night in which he was betrayed took bread: and when he had given thanks, he brake it . . . ' Here the phrase 'when he had given thanks' represents only a single word in the Greek original, the word *eucharistesas*. Thus the central rite of the Christian liturgy is a rite of gratitude. It is also a rite and liturgy of remembrance, for our Lord went on to say, 'This do in remembrance of me.' But we remember in order to give thanks, as is already made plain in the Old Testament where it is in psalms of thanksgiving that we come upon such declarations as 'I will remember the works of the Lord.' And what is thus true of the Christian worship is also true of the whole Christian life. It is a life of remembrance which issues in thanksgiving. A true Christian is a man who never for a moment forgets what God has done for him in Christ, and whose whole comportment and whole activity have their root in the sentiment of gratitude . . .

The perfection of Christian saintliness is that we should be enabled to thank God even for the worst troubles that come to us, including death, realizing that their ultimate purpose is to bring us closer to himself, and that without them we cannot be made perfect.[1]

I wish for you the joy of Christmas and the best New Year ever.

John H. Leith

---

1. Baillie, *The Sense of the Presence of God*, 237, 238.

# 6

## Christmas 1978

WILLIAM TEMPLE writes this about Christmas:

Above all the overwhelming splendour the Gospel of Christmas consists in precisely this—that the Lord of glory of His own will entered into our life of grief and suffering, and for love of men bore all and more than all that men may be called to bear. It is this fact which leads us to say that love came down at Christmas. If all that happened was that a baby was born who would grow up to be a wonderful teacher, then Christmas takes its place among the birthdays of great men; it is not then the festival of divine love. Of course this central Christian belief baffles intellect and holds imagination fascinated. It is either true or false; it is not to be thought of chiefly as beautiful, or inspiring, or comforting. The first question to be asked is— Is it true or false? for much of its beauty and all its power to comfort or inspire comes from its truth. And then how overwhelming the wonder is—

> That the Great Angell-blinding light should shrinke
> His blaze, to shine in a poore Shepherd's eye;
> That the unmeasur'd God so low should sinke,
> As Pris'ner in a few poore Rags to ly;

That from his Mother's Brest he milke should
   drinke,
Who feeds with Nectar Heav'ns faire family,
   That a vile Manger his low Bed should prove,
   Who in a Throne of stars Thunders above;

That he whom the Sun serves, should faintly
   peepe
Through clouds of Infant flesh! that he, the old
Eternall Word should be a Child, and weepe;
That he who made the fire, should feare the
   cold,
That Heav'ns high Majesty his Court should
   keepe
In a clay cottage, by each blast control'd;
   That Glories self should serve our Griefs
      and feares,
   And free Eternity submit to yeares.

It is this tremendous faith that can nerve us to
the conquest of the evil in the world and carry us
forward to the better order which all long to see.
"This is the victory which overcometh the world,
even our faith. . . ."

But if God, the Almighty and Eternal God, has
shared our experience in its depths of weakness
and pain, and out of this has won a power that
increasingly lays hold of men's hearts and wills,
not overriding their freedom but using it as the
way of approach to the citadel of their being, then
there is hope. We do not have to conquer this evil
world in any strength of ours; in spite of its brave
showing, it is a beaten thing; and if we treat so,
in our own hearts or in the world outside, it will
crack and crumple and dissolve.[1]

---

1. Temple, *The Church Looks Forward*, 98–99.

May this be a very merry Christmas for you and the happiest New Year ever. May the New Year be theologically productive, and may the church, Union Theological Seminary, and the faith be in various ways our true home.

John H. Leith

# 7

# Christmas 1979

Karl Barth has said, as have many others, that the bottom line in Christian faith is trusting God in life and in death. Hence, one of the best Christmas greetings is those remarkable words from Matthew 6:25–34:

> "Therefore I tell you, do not be anxious about your life, what you shall eat or what you shall drink, nor about your body, what you shall put on. Is not life more than food, and the body more than clothing? Look at the birds of the air: they neither sow nor reap nor gather into barns, and yet your heavenly Father feeds them. Are you not of more value than they? And which of you by being anxious can add one cubit to his span of life? And why are you anxious about clothing? Consider the lilies of the field, how they grow; they neither toil nor spin; yet I tell you, even Solomon in all his glory was not arrayed like one of these. But if God so clothes the grass of the field, which today is alive and tomorrow is thrown into the oven, will he not much more clothe you, O men of little faith? Therefore do not be anxious, saying, 'What shall we eat?' or 'What shall we drink?' or 'What shall we wear?' For the Gentiles seek all these things; and your

heavenly Father knows that you need them all.
But seek first his kingdom and his righteousness,
and all these things shall be yours as well.

"Therefore do not be anxious about tomorrow,
for tomorrow will be anxious for itself. Let the
day's own trouble be sufficient for the day."

I hope this Christmas that all of us who have shared
life at Union Theological Seminary and in the theological
work of the church will also share the blessing of this trust
and confidence.

John H. Leith

# 8

## Christmas 1980

THIS CHRISTMAS greeting goes to friends whom I have known as students of theology and now as colleagues in the ministry. It is appropriate that these relationships established at Union Theological Seminary should be renewed at Christmas. The only greeting is the old greeting, but I will share three very different quotations that have caught my attention.

### "In Place of a Curse"

At the next vacancy for God, if I am elected,
I shall forgive last the delicately wounded
who, having been slugged no harder than anyone else,
never got up again, neither to fight back,
nor to finger their jaws in painful admiration.

They who are wholly broken, and they in whom
mercy is understanding, I shall embrace at once
and lead to pillows in heaven. But they who are
the meek by trade, baiting the best of their betters
with the extortions of a mock-helplessness

I shall take last to love, and never wholly.
Let them all into Heaven—I abolish Hell—
but let it be read over them as they enter:

"Beware the calculations of the meek, who gambled
    nothing,
gave nothing, and could never receive enough."[1]

## "A Carol for Children"

God rest you, merry Innocents,
Let nothing you dismay,
Let nothing wound an eager heart
Upon this Christmas day. . . .

Soon, soon enough come crueler gifts,
The anger and the tears;
Between you now there sparsely drifts
A handful yet of years. . . .

Two ultimate laws alone we know,
The ledger and the sword—
So far away, so long ago,
We lost the infant Lord.

Only children clasp his hand;
His voice speaks low to them,
And still for them the shining band
Wings over Bethlehem.

God rest you, merry Innocents,
While innocence endures. . . .[2]

1. John Ciardi, "In Place of a Curse," 13.

2. Ogden Nash, "A Carol for Children," 218. See Christmas 1998,
"When the Angels Went Away, What Then?" and Christmas 1999
below.

## "I Call Myself a Christian"

I call myself a Christian though there are those who challenge my right to that name, either because they require a Christian to maintain some one of various sets of beliefs that I do not hold or because they require him to live up to some one of various sets of moral standards, including those of my own conscience, to which I do not conform. I call myself a Christian simply because I also am a follower of Jesus Christ, though I travel at a great distance from him not only in time but in the spirit of my traveling; because I believe that my way of thinking about life, myself, my human companions and our destiny has been so modified by his presence in our history that I cannot get away from his influence; and also because I do not want to get away from it; above all, I call myself a Christian because my relation to God has been, so far as I can see, deeply conditioned by this presence of Jesus Christ in my history and in our history. In one sense I must call myself a Christian in the same way that I call myself a twentieth-century man. To be a Christian is simply part of my fate. . . . But I call myself a Christian more because I have both accepted this fateful fact and because I identify myself with what I understand to be the cause of Jesus Christ. That cause I designate simply as the reconciliation of man to God.[3]

Merry Christmas and a happy New Year!

John H. Leith

3. H. Richard Niebuhr, *Responsible Self*, 43.

# 9

# Christmas 1981

PERHAPS IT is age; perhaps it is the tragedy of the so-called "creationist-evolutionist" debate in which each side is frighteningly wrong; perhaps it is the lost sense of mystery and wonder in contemporary life; perhaps on a better level it is the reading of "newer" (for me) theologians, such as Karl Rahner, as well as older theologians, such as Reinhold Niebuhr; perhaps it is reading the anthropologists and the astronomers, especially Jastrow; but this Christmas confronts us with the questionableness of existence or the presence of mystery. The "questionableness" as well as the "mystery" break through all the protective devices our culture uses to isolate life from its source or its destiny.

Richard Hocking has told that his father, W. E. Hocking, one of America's most distinguished philosophers, would weep as he read to his family the Christmas story from Luke. He was overcome by the wonder of it all.

John Eccles, the Nobel prize laureate, when selected to give the Gifford lectures, deliberately chose the title *The Human Mystery*. Here are some sentences from those remarkable lectures:

The tremendous successes of science in the last century have led to the expectation that there will be forthcoming in the near future a complete explanation in materialist terms of all the fundamental problems confronting us. These "great questions," as they are called, have exercised the creative thinkers from Greek times onwards. It has been fashionable to overplay the explanatory power of science and this has led to the regrettable reactions of anti-science and of all manner of irrationalistic and magical beliefs. When confronted with the frightening assertion by scientists that we are no more than participants in the materialist happenings of chance and necessity, anti-science is a natural reaction. . . .

It is my thesis that we have to recognize the unique selfhood as being the result of a supernatural creation of what in the religious sense is called a soul. . . .

Overarching all the expression and argument of this lecture series is the insight that each of us is a participant in some great mysterious drama, as Sherrington and Schrödinger believed.

The profound tragedy of our age is that this religious vision has become dimmed or rejected.[1]

In the presence of mystery, the Christmas faith is awesome. "The Word became flesh and dwelt among us, full of grace and truth" (John 1:14).

John H. Leith

1. John Eccles, *Human Mystery*, 8–9, 144, 236.

# Christmas 1982

Q UOTING THEOLOGY has grown into a habit as a greeting to those I have known in the study of theology at Union Theological Seminary. Some may consider this a dull practice, but for those who are excited by theology it remains the best I can do.

This past year the books that have meant the most to me have been Goppelt, *Theology of the New Testament*; Robert A. Markus, *Saeculum: History and Society in the Theology of Augustine*; Otto Weber, *Foundation of Dogmatics*; and Herbert Butterfield, *The Origins of History* and *Writings on Christianity and History*. The following quotations are from *Writings on Christianity and History*:

> People forget that the grand fact of European history is the constant preaching of the gospel, the conversion of souls to a more authentic appropriation of religion, and the ministering to their spiritual necessities—a thing which the historian can hardly go on repeating, though it is the same year after year and generation after generation. Here is the impressive story, the point where the work of the Church has eternal validity; here is the task in which it has never failed, the task in which it must not be thought to have failed

even when many men are turning their backs upon religion. We often do an injustice both to Churches and to Churchmen because we hold a skeleton of politico-ecclesiastical history in our minds and fail to picture the life of the clergy in its intimacy and its fullness.

I happen to have known a number of people— two of them amongst the ablest men I ever knew, but two of them who never had any schooling after the age of ten, one of them a woman who never read anything apart from the Bible, except a very popular paper called the *Sunday Companion*—and they seem to me to have reached the real secret of life and touched the bottom of things in a way that makes me feel the world of forlorn clever rudderless dons quite a superficial affair. I could not convince anybody else but I am convinced myself that these people walked with God, and there are a lot of them in history—these people who were sure of their contact with the living Christ. The historian has to admit the extraordinary power that this had over their personalities and lives.

Three things, however, seem to illustrate the importance of Christianity in that mundane history which is under discussion—the importance of the particular religion which presided over the rise of what we call our Western civilisation. They all spring from the very nature of the Christian gospel itself and their effects on our civilisation are merely the incidental results of the ordinary religious activity of the Church—they are not a sample or a vindication of the mundane policies of ecclesiastics. They are by-products of the missionary and spiritual work of the Church, and it is not clear that the same mundane benefits would accrue if men set out with the object of procuring the mundane benefits—if men worked with their eyes on the by-products themselves. They show that the Church has best served civilisation not on the occasions when it had civilisation as its conscious object, but when it was most intent on the salvation of souls and most content to leave the rest to Providence. The three things are the leavening effect of Christian charity, the assertion of the autonomy of spiritual principle, and the insistence on the spiritual character of personality. Apart from the softening effect that religion often (but perhaps not always) has had on manners and morals, these things have had their influences on the very texture of our Western civilisation.

What the Christian affirmation really involves, therefore, is the insistence that life in the world is capable of a further dimension which many people leave out of account. We all understand that man has a life that can be lived on an intellectual plane, transcending mere animal existence, though I suspect that if we had looked at this globe some millions of years ago none of us would have believed that even that was possible. None of us would have believed that lumps of matter could ever have stood up in the world (as we do) and asked what it was all about, ask what they were doing there. We all understand that man has a status not only as an intellectual but also as a moral creature, though this would not necessarily have anything to do with religion, since morality itself is often held to possess merely a mundane reference. The Christian challenge, however, has meant the assertion of a further dimension to the universe and to human life itself—a spiritual order of existence in which men have felt that they walked with God and had communion with the living Christ. Religion may need continual reformulation and restatement, but we are not permitted to evaporate that spiritual element out of it. And the ultimate intellectual problem is the question of the validity of the spiritual experience. Churches are sometimes dangerous things, and, unless they are very spiritual indeed they can actually be a harmful influence in a country. But where they are unique, where they really stand or fall, is in their assertion of an additional dimension to life—this communion with the living Christ, this insistence on the actual practise of the spiritual life.[1]

I hope Christmas will be a wonderful experience for you and the New Year will be the best ever.

John H. Leith

---

1. Butterfield, *Writings on Christianity and History*, 207–8, 267, 167, 257–58.

# Christmas 1983

M ODERN TIMES by Paul Johnson is the most informa-
tive, stimulating and provocative new book I read in
1983. A central thesis is the following paragraph:

> Marx described a world in which the central
> dynamic was economic interest. To Freud, the
> principal thrust was sexual. Both assumed that
> religion, the old impulse which moved men
> and masses, was a fantasy and always had been.
> Friedrich Nietzsche, the third of the trio, was also
> an atheist. But he saw God not as an invention but
> as a casualty, and his demise as in some impor-
> tant sense an historical event, which would have
> dramatic consequences. He wrote in 1886: 'The
> great event of recent times—that "God is dead,"
> that the belief in the Christian God is no longer
> tenable—is beginning to cast its first shadows
> over Europe.' Among the advanced races, the de-
> cline and ultimately the collapse of the religious
> impulse would leave a huge vacuum. The history
> of modern times is in great part the history of
> how that vacuum had been filled. Nietzsche
> rightly perceived that the most likely candidate
> would be what he called the 'Will to Power,'
> which offered a far more comprehensive and in

the end more plausible explanation of human behaviour than either Marx or Freud. In place of religious belief, there would be secular ideology. Those who had once filled the ranks of the totalitarian clergy would become totalitarian politicians. And, above all, the Will to Power would produce a new kind of messiah, uninhibited by any religious sanctions whatever, and with an unappeasable appetite for controlling mankind. The end of the old order, with an unguided world adrift in a relativistic universe, was a summons to such gangster-statesmen to emerge. They were not slow to make their appearance.[1]

The thesis applies to the church. When God is absent and the gospel is dead, we become terribly busy with trivia. We become passionate about organization, about management, about ecclesiastical power, even about revising the curriculum. We no longer read serious theology or give theological answers to human questions. And the church as a community of faith withers.

Christmas is a reminder that the most important message ever to come to human beings on this planet is the good news: "The Word became flesh and dwelt among us." (John 1:14) A lifetime is too short to understand it all. The maximum of human energy is inadequate to proclaim it. No other task is so crucial.

I wish you the joy and peace of Christmas and the best New Year ever.

John H. Leith

---

1. Johnson, *Modern Times*, 48.

# Christmas 1984

D URING THE year I collected brief quotations for this Christmas greeting from the new books I *enjoyed* reading:

Thomas Peters and Robert H. Waterman, *In Search of Excellence*;

Stanley L. Jaki, *Angels, Apes, and Men*;

John Eccles and Daniel N. Robinson, *The Wonder of Being Human*; and

James J. Kilpatrick, *The Writer's Art*.

When time came to prepare the letter and after the experience of the election and the religion and politics debate,[1] I decided on the seventeenth paragraph of Book XIX of one of the greatest books of all time, Augustine's *City of God*.

This paragraph is appropriate, I think, not only because it speaks to our time, but primarily because it embodies so much of the faith that unites us personally and also in our work in the Christian community.

1. In 1984, Ronald Reagan was overwhelmingly reelected to the presidency.

The families which do not live by faith seek their peace in the earthly advantages of this life; while the families which live by faith look for those eternal blessings which are promised, and use as pilgrims such advantages of time and of earth as do not fascinate and divert them from God, but rather aid them to endure with greater ease, and to keep down the number of those burdens of the corruptible body which weigh upon the soul. Thus the things necessary for this mortal life are used by both kinds of men and families alike, but each has its own peculiar and widely different aim in using them.

The earthly city, which does not live by faith, seeks an earthly peace, and the end it proposes, in the well-ordered concord of civic obedience and rule, is the combination of men's wills to attain the things which are helpful to this life. The heavenly city, or rather the part of it which sojourns on earth and lives by faith, makes use of this peace only because it must, until this mortal condition which necessitates it shall pass away. Consequently, so long as it lives like a captive and a stranger in the earthly city, though it has already received the promise of redemption, and the gift of the Spirit as the earnest of it, it makes no scruple to obey the laws of the earthly city, whereby the things necessary for the maintenance of this mortal life are administered; and thus, as this life is common to both cities, so there is a harmony between them in regard to what belongs to it.

But, as the earthly city has had some philosophers whose doctrine is condemned by the divine teaching, and who, being deceived either by their own conjectures or by demons, supposed that many gods must be invited to take an interest in human affairs, and assigned to each a separate function and a separate department . . . the celestial city, on the other hand, knew that one God only was to be worshipped, and that to Him alone was due that service which the Greeks call *latreia*, and which can be given only to a god, it has come to pass that the two cities could not have common laws of religion, and that the heavenly city has been compelled in this matter to dissent, and to become obnoxious to those who think differently, and to stand the brunt of their anger and hatred and persecutions, except in so far as the minds of their enemies have been alarmed by the multitude of the Christians and quelled by the manifest protection of God accorded to them. This heavenly city, then, while it sojourns on earth, calls citizens out of all nations, and gathers together a society of pilgrims of all languages, not scrupling about diversities in the manners, laws, and institutions whereby earthly peace is secured and maintained, but recognizing that, however various these are, they all tend to one and the same end of earthly peace. It therefore is so far from rescinding and abolishing these diversities, that it even preserves and adopts them, so long only as no hindrance to the worship of the one supreme and true God is thus introduced.

Even the heavenly city, therefore, while in its state of pilgrimage, avails itself of the peace of earth, and, so far as it can without injuring faith and godliness, desires and maintains a common agreement among men regarding the acquisition of the necessaries of life, and makes this earthly peace bear upon the peace of heaven; for this alone can be truly called and esteemed the peace of the reasonable creatures, consisting as it does in the perfectly ordered and harmonious enjoyment of God and of one another in God. When we shall have reached that peace, this mortal life shall give place to one that is eternal, and our body shall be no more this animal body which by its corruption weighs down the soul, but a spiritual body feeling no want, and in all its members subjected to the will. In its pilgrim state the heavenly city possesses this peace by faith; and by this faith it lives righteously when it refers to the attainment of that peace every good action towards God and man; for the life of the city is a social life.[2]

May this be a wonderful Christmas and the best New Year ever.

John H. Leith

2. Augustine, *City of God*, 412–13.

# 13

# Christmas 1985

WE HAVE made Christmas a celebration of creation, but this is possible only because it is first a celebration of the grace of God in our redemption. Hence, I know no better greeting for those of us whose friendship began in the study of theology and has been nurtured by theological commitments than some paragraphs from "The Rule of Grace," a lecture given to the Uniting Church of Australia by Albert Outler, in some ways the best teacher I ever knew and always an eloquent, brilliant and persistent preacher of the Christian faith. The Rule of Grace has to do not only with us personally but with the way of the church in the world.

> Christians are "under grace," and this is the energy and essence of all their special virtues of gratitude and love. . . . "The rule of grace" is human life as it may be lived here and now, under Christ's reign, come and coming (cf. the reference to the "reign of Christ" [*regnum Christi*] in 1 Corinthians 15:25, Ephesians 5:5, Colossians 1:13, Hebrews 12:28, 2 Timothy 2:12, 2 Peter 1:11, Revelation 1:9; 11:15). Christ's reign is the alternative to all the other orders and disorders in which human beings have tried to live: all

those flawed reigns of instinct and coercion, of "law" and self-indulgence. . . .

In the New Testament, grace is typically identified as "the grace of Christ." "The Rule of Christ" is, therefore, an equivalent for the notion of "the rule of grace." In the early church, grace was understood as God's holy purpose to restore fallen humanity to its primal state: "the image and similitude of God" (Genesis 1:26). This was conceived of as a gracious intercommunion between divine and human (*metousia Theou*). The active energy in this restoration is Christ's redeeming work, in its entirety. This was the sole and sufficient meritorious cause of our salvation, which none could have merited. Ethically, then, grace is the triumph of God's mercy over his bare justice, the burden of which is intolerable even to the best of us. . . .

Jesus reminded his disciples how the "rulers" among the Gentiles loved to lord it over their underlings. But what he feared then came to pass: Christian "rulers" also came to love lording it over their "underlings," to cherish the symbols and perquisites of "office" and "authority." We Protestants are quick to see this in the hierarchical polities of the Roman Catholics; how, for example, the pope is *Pontifex Maximus Romae* (a residual secular title), how much longer the *capa magna* of a cardinal than a mere archbishop's! We are less sensitive to the strong family resemblance between our secular and ecclesiastical politics, and the "Byzantine mentality" in our bureaucrats, or even to our minorities under the occasional tyrannies of "majority rule." Indeed, the normal connotation of "minority" in common speech focuses on ethnic groups. We rarely think about the ways in which decisions voted by majorities in our assemblies sometimes oppress the consciences of those outvoted. The glaring equivalences between ecclesiastical lustings for power and the half-cynical power-games we play in church administration have had disastrous consequences for our credibility in the world, and yet only our aggrieved dissidents "prophesy" against them. A church that speaks of grace and relies on power is not likely to do more than bemuse "the world." The "kingdom of God and his righteousness" is equally unconcerned with coercion, on the one hand, or sentimentality, on the other. It proclaims a rule of righteousness in which the essence of "righteousness" (justice!) is "grace." God is in his heaven; his sovereignty is secure; he does rule "the world with truth and grace." . . .

Indeed, the human struggle for humanity is doomed to self-defeat save where it is a manifestation of the rule of grace, acknowledged or unacknowledged. If we cannot boast of any notable successes in bringing in the kingdom here on earth, the record of all the alternatives has been worse. We know (or ought to know) how revolutions devour their own children, how the displacements of one power block by another, in societies oriented to the principle of self-advantage, result in new tyrannies, new injustices. We ought also to know, by now, how utopias stir false hopes and them betray them. If, on the other hand, we probed more deeply into personal and social dynamisms in history and in our own lives, we would be able to see that grace, even where it does not rule unchallenged, has been (and still is) an active power in the salvaging of human values from the dehumanising powers in this world. It is less than a panacea in a fallen world, but it is far more than a dream or abstraction.

The kingdom of God (the rule of grace) is "at-hand." Repent and believe this "good news." It is not an easy gospel to believe, and our repentance (i.e. our turning away from patterns of self-advantage) comes hard. This is why, from the beginning until now, the greatest hindrance to the kingdom's coming is unbelief: our unwillingness or inability to believe that God's righteousness and grace can dwell in our hearts by faith and that, even in this world with all its agonies and distractions, we really can "know the love of Christ, which exceeds all rational knowledge, and come to be filled with the fulness of God himself" (Ephesians 3:17–21). For that is the end and aim of the rule of grace, and its promises are still as valid for us and for humanity as ever they were. "Repent and believe this good news": this is still humanity's choice (and ours), between life and death in God or life and death in alienation.

It was a mild culture shock to learn that, for reasons largely "non-theological," John Newton's great hymn about "Amazing Grace" is not a favorite in current Australian hymnody. Even so, I am still inclined to urge its theological thesis upon you, as a reconsideration of a vital old tradition. "Twas grace that taught my heart to fear" (which is to say that grace stirs the conscience to true repentance); "And grace my fears relieved" (by conversion that led to reconciliation); "Through many a danger, toils and snares" (each of us has a special catalogue of these) "we have already come" (without quite knowing how); "Twas grace hath brought us safe thus far" (it is the only perspective in which church history can be read with profit); "And grace will lead us home" (Gordon Rupp's point in his familiar phrase "the optimism of grace").

The sum of it all is that we should seek to see in the rich mysteries of grace the ground and ordering influence in our lives and in the human course, past and future![1]

I hope you a joyous Christmas and the best New Year ever.

John H. Leith

---

1. Outler, *Rule of Grace*, 14, 15, 16–17, 21–22.

# 14

# Christmas 1986

I WISH for each one who receives this greeting the best Christmas and the happiest New Year ever. Christmas reminds us not only of the origin of our faith but of the common life we share in that faith, which I like to call—though it is embarrassing and presumptuous to do so—the communion of saints. For this community, sharing a common faith, life, and hope, we give thanks at Christmas.

The greeting below is from a book which has commanded my attention for the past year. One may quibble with certain points, yet it is the best recent book in my judgment on the state of theology in this country. It is appropriate to read it at Christmas, for the Word made flesh challenges the pervasive ethos of American life and even of many churches.

For some the Word made flesh is foolishness. It is either unnecessary or impossible, as there is no Word anyhow, or both.

For some the Word made flesh is a scandal. The Jews found Jesus Christ a scandal. The Christ who came was not the Christ they expected. Our pluralistic, secular culture finds Christ a scandal; for if a revelatory word become flesh, this Word cannot be the only Word. The Word made flesh is at best relative to other words.

For us this Christmas, there can be no greater celebration than to proclaim again that the Word became flesh and dwelt among us, full of grace and truth.

## "Unbelief in America"

Within twenty years after the Civil War, agnosticism emerged as a self-sustaining phenomenon. Disbelief in God was, for the first time, plausible enough to grow beyond a rare eccentricity and to stake out a sizable permanent niche in American culture. Two hundred years spent adopting belief to the cultural environment had paid off, in a way: unbelief now also fitted tolerably well into it—well enough to find sufficient intellectual and psychological nourishment to survive and reproduce itself. An agnostic subculture had taken root—not a geographic community, but a community of ideas, assumptions, and values. This shared world view gave agnostics a coherent understanding of reality without benefit of God. That their world view was shared reinforced their agnosticism, for they knew that many others, and not insignificant men, agreed with their doubts. That it was a subculture—that agnosticism was broadly continuous with the fundamental assumptions of the larger culture—made their unbelief convincing. For agnosticism did not represent a sharp break from Victorian culture, but rather one plausible outgrowth of it. . . .

The crucial ingredient, then, in the mix that produced an enduring unbelief was the choices of believers. More precisely, unbelief resulted from the decisions that influential church leaders— lay writers, theologians, ministers—made about how to confront the modern pressures upon religious belief. Not all of their selections resulted from long thought and careful reflection; part of our humanity, after all, is that we have much in common with lemmings. But they were choices. And the choices, taken together, boiled down to a decision to deal with modernity by embracing it—to defuse modern threats to the traditional bases of belief by bringing God into line with modernity.

In tailoring belief more closely to human understanding and aspiration, however, many religious leaders made a fatal slip. They were not wrong to think than any significant faith would have to express itself in moral practice. But they often forgot that their God's purposes were not supposed to be man's. They were not mistaken in believing that any resilient belief must ground itself in human thought and experience. But they frequently forgot the tension that, by definition, must exist between an incomprehensible God and the human effort to know Him. They were hardly fools to insist that any God must be lord of this world, but they did not always remember that this world could not define Him. They forgot, in short, that their God was—as any God had to be to command belief over the long term—radically other than man.

Put slightly differently, unbelief emerged because church leaders too often forgot the transcendence essential to any worthwhile God. They committed religion *functionally* to making the world better in human terms and *intellectually* to modes of knowing God fitted only for understanding this world. They did this because, trying to meet the challenge of modernity, they virtually surrendered to it. These ministers and theologians well understood that belief could not continue in its old tracks. They did not grasp firmly enough that it did not simply have to jump to the new, that belief could modify secular wisdom in the very process of adapting to it. . . .

Yet perhaps, after all, there is really only one lesson here. The universe is not tailored to our measurements. Forgetting that, many believers lost their God. So may we all run into trouble.[1]

This is "heavy" and disturbing reading. Hence, I am enclosing a copy of a Christmas writing of Halford Luccock. It, too, is disturbing—so much that I remember first reading it almost forty years ago.

John H. Leith

---

1. Turner, *Without God, Without Creed*, 171–72, 266–67, 269.

## CHRISTMAS DAY IN THE MORNING

EDITOR THE CHRISTIAN CENTURY:

Sir: Of all the Christmas celebrations I ever heard of, two stick like burrs in my memory. No carols, no holly, no Christmas trees or sleigh bells. But Christmas parties just the same.

The first was on Christmas morning 1809, at Danville, Kentucky, on the edge of the wilderness. A young physician, Ephraim McDowell, who had come into Kentucky only two jumps behind Daniel Boone, was preparing for a surgical operation in which he not only risked the life of his patient but also took his own life in his hands. Mrs. Thomas Crawford had made an agonizing journey of sixty miles on horseback to see if her life could be saved. To save her required an abdominal operation of a sort that had never before been performed in all medical history. It meant cutting into the abdominal cavity, which then, all over the world, was labeled plain murder. Yet this backwoods doctor, his only equipment a plain wooden table, on which the patient was strapped, stood ready to do what no man had ever dared before.

Outside the house an angry mob had gathered and thrown a rope over the limb of a tree, ready to hang Dr. McDowell if the patient died. But he counted not life dear unto himself. He went ahead, and the patient lived. That operation was the forerunner of a major part of modern surgery. James Thomas Flexner says, "Every operation for appendicitis or gall stones since is a lineal descendant of one daring experiment in the wilderness of Kentucky." A Christmas gift!

Drop down the calendar about a hundred years, to 1900. It is now Christmas Day in the morning in Santiago, Cuba. There a private soldier in the United States army, John J. Moran (a name that deserves more remembrance than it has received), celebrated Christmas by coming down with a whopping case of yellow fever, every symptom perfect. Yellow fever did not just happen to Private Moran; he asked for it. He offered his life as a test of the theory which Dr. Walter Reed and others were working on, that yellow fever was transmitted by mosquitoes. Four days earlier Moran had entered a closed room and voluntarily played host to a swarm of mosquitoes that had been feasting on yellow fever patients. Early on Christmas morning he entered the valley of the shadow of death. After a long siege he recovered, and brought back with him the indisputable proof of the cause of yellow fever—the truth that has practically wiped yellow fever off the map of the world.

Not very Christmasy stories, these. No atmosphere, no off-stage music. Or was there music? Perhaps the herald angels did sing. At any rate, these are stories of a fitting celebration of the birthday of One who came to give his life a ransom for many.

The same to you and many of them!

Simeon Stylites[2]

2. Luccock, "Christmas Day in the Morning," 1392.

# 15

# Christmas 1987

CHRISTMAS BRINGS us tidings of great joy. The Word became flesh. It is also the occasion of great joy in the community created by the birth, life, death and resurrection of Jesus Christ.

Christmas greetings belong to the community of saints. Hence it is an increasing joy to send a Christmas greeting to those who share with me a common life at Union Theological Seminary and, more than that, common purposes and understandings in the work of the ministry.

I intended to read last summer two books that were not in the specific field of theology. I did not finish Sidney Hook's biography, but I did greatly enjoy reading Allan Bloom's *The Closing of the American Mind*. I wish he had written it better; but even when I didn't agree, I admired the intensity and courage with which he stated his views. Much of what he wrote could have been written about churches and seminaries, as well as universities. I am quoting two very interesting paragraphs:

> The cause of this decay of the family's traditional role as the transmitter of tradition is the same as that of the decay of the humanities: nobody believes that the old books do, or even could, contain the truth. So books have become, at

best, "culture," i.e., boring. As Tocqueville put it, in a democracy tradition is nothing more than information. With the "information explosion," tradition has become superfluous. As soon as tradition has come to be recognized as tradition, it is dead, something to which lip service is paid in the vain hope of edifying the kids. In the United States, practically speaking, the Bible was the only common culture, one that united simple and sophisticated, rich and poor, young and old, and—as the very model for a vision of the order of the whole of things, as well as the key to the rest of Western art, the greatest works of which were in one way or another responsive to the Bible—provided access to the seriousness of books. With its gradual and inevitable disappearance, the very idea of such a total book and the possibility and necessity of world-explanation is disappearing. And fathers and mothers have lost the idea that the highest aspiration they might have for their children is for them to be wise—as priests, prophets or philosophers are wise. Specialized competence and success are all that they can imagine. Contrary to what is commonly thought, without the book even the idea of the order of the whole is lost. . . .

I am distinguishing two related but different problems here. The contents of the classic books have become particularly difficult to defend in modern times, and the professors who now teach them do not care to defend them, are not interested in their truth. One can most clearly see the latter in the case of the Bible. To include it in the humanities is already a blasphemy, a denial of its own claims. There it is almost inevitably treated in one of two ways: It is subjected to modern "scientific" analysis, called the Higher Criticism, where it is dismantled, to show how "sacred" books are put together, and that they are not what they claim to be. It is useful as a mosaic in which on finds the footprints of many dead civilizations. Or else the Bible is used in courses in comparative religion as the one expression of the need for the "sacred" and as a contribution to the very modern, very scientific study of the structure of "myths." (Here one can join up with the anthropologists and really be alive.) A teacher who treated the Bible naively, taking it at its word, or Word, would be accused of scientific incompetence and lack of sophistication. Moreover, he might rock the boat and start the religious wars all over again, as well as a quarrel within the university between reason and revelation, which would upset comfortable arrangements and wind up by being humiliating to the humanities. Here one sees the traces of the Enlightenment's political project, which wanted precisely to render the Bible, and other old books, undangerous. This project is one of the underlying causes of the impotence of the humanities. The best that can be done, it appears, is to teach "The Bible as Literature," as opposed to "as Revelation," which it claims to be. In this way it can be read somewhat independently of deforming scholarly apparatus, as we read, for example, *Pride and Prejudice.* Thus the few professors who feel that there is something wrong with the other approaches tend to their consciences.[1]

---

1. Bloom, *Closing of the American Mind*, 58, 374–75.

I hope for you the authentic joy of Christmas and a New Year that will bring satisfaction. I look forward to the next year in the church, because I am more and more persuaded of the power of preaching, teaching and pastoral care, when blessed by the Holy Spirit, to build up the church. I am more and more convinced of the folly of putting so much emphasis on reorganization, liturgical reform, being relevant and other practices that demonstrably do not build up congregations. I have great hope for the future of the Presbyterian and Reformed way of being Christian, because of what so many who receive this greeting are doing.

John H. Leith

# 16

# Christmas 1988

JOHN CALVIN once chided Genevans for turning out in greater numbers for worship on Christmas Day. His discipline of the Christian life did not need a Christian calendar. Yet Christmas serves very useful purposes. First, it is the occasion for Christmas greetings, which help to maintain community in a highly mobile society. Second, Christmas is an occasion not only for gifts given out of duty. It also inspires spontaneity in our generosity which we seldom duplicate. Finally, and most important, Christmas turns our attention to the Christian fact and doctrine that God became man for our salvation.

> In the beginning was the Word, and the Word was with God, and the Word was God. He was in the beginning with God; all things were made through him, and without him was not anything made that was made. . . .
>
> And the Word became flesh and dwelt among us, full of grace and truth; we have beheld his glory, glory as of the only Son from the Father. . . . No one has ever seen God; the only Son, who is in the bosom of the Father, he has made him known.[1]

1. John 1:1–3, 14, 18.

Christians first celebrated the birth of Jesus on December 25th in the fourth century, setting the remembrance of the birth of Jesus on the occasion of a festival that celebrated the vitalities and energies of nature. Today we observe Christmas not only amid a popular paganism that finds the meaning of life in the intensification of the vitalities and energies of life, but also in a social situation that is highly pluralistic.

Christmas confronts us with the serious theological responsibility of relating the words of John to the pluralism of our society. A sociologist, John Murray Cuddihy, published a book some ten years ago entitled *No Offense: Civil Religion and Protestant Taste*, arguing that civil religion has become the religion of civility.

Christmas today may be foolishness to many, but the theological scandal is diminished. Indeed, for some, the removal of the scandal has become the kerygma.

All those who take Christmas seriously, must discover ways to affirm the great and wondrous truth that the Word became flesh and yet to affirm it without triumphalism, without self-righteousness, without fanaticism. Tolerance that combines convictions deeply and passionately held with respect for the integrity of other persons who do not share our convictions is a possibility. It is this possibility that makes a democratic and pluralistic society possible, but it is pluralism that puts at risk the very dogma that makes tolerance, rather than indifference possible. There is no dogma without an anathema; yet the anathema need not be one of fanaticism. The Christmas story itself has a plainness, a simplicity that is compelling without being arrogant or triumphal.

Albert Outler is a theologian who has never wavered in his conviction that the Word became flesh, who has given expression to this conviction with grace. These words of his from a sermon on John 3:16 are a very appropriate Christmas greeting in 1988:

> In and with Jesus of Nazareth, we have to do with the Living God, in grace and power—nothing less. . . .
>
> But we will never understand the drama as a whole, in any scope or depth, until we have understood its central character. This is why our faith in *Jesus Christ* must search out and reach for an adequate understanding. *This* is what Christology is all about—as adequate an understanding as we can manage of the mystery of the One who was truly human as any of us and yet also truly divine. This is, indeed, an inexhaustible mystery. But there are better and worse ways of understanding it, and it makes a crucial difference for Christian *living* that the *better* ways be sorted out from the worse. . . .
>
> But the quality of any *analysis* depends upon what is to be analyzed—and in Christian experience, this must be the living faith of Christians in Jesus Christ as Lord and Savior to the glory of God the Father. This is the faith that has been summed up in our text—and in its mate in Second Corinthians 5:
>
>> For God so loved the world—and so loved *us*—that he gave his first-born Son, that whosoever believes in him [faiths him, puts life and destiny in his hands and grace] shall not perish, but have life ever-

> lasting. For God was in Christ reconciling the world to himself. *Therefore, be reconciled to God* through Christ—not only to be saved, but to live in the world as Christ lived in the days of his flesh.[2]

Cuddihy speaks of "The Homely Protestant: A Decorum of Imperfection."[3] The New Testament tells us Jesus came to call sinners, not the righteous, to repentance. It is as poor sinners we have to say, to sing, to proclaim, "Joy to the world! the Lord is come." There is the decorum of sinners saved by grace. Yet this Christmas, let us remember, the unostentatious, meek sinners of the New Testament dared to die for their faith and to witness to its truth before the rulers and wise people of this world.

May this be for you a wonderful Christmas and may the New Year be the best ever.

John H. Leith

2. Outler, *Preacher*, 225, 230. In an introduction on page 223, the editor notes, "This sermon was given as an Auburn University Leith Lecture on October 25, 1983."

3. Cuddihy, *No Offense*, 191.

# 17

# Christmas 1989

THIS CHRISTMAS greeting is to wish for you the joy that Jesus Christ brings—the joy of creation and the joy of redemption.

It also brings the New Year's hope that God's purposes shall be fulfilled in our lives and in society with a grace that we cannot now imagine.

A greeting at the end of more than thirty years of teaching has to be a remembrance of how much each one who receives it has meant to the fullness of my life. The Colloquium last April[1] was a reminder of how much I am indebted to so many people, as well as an assurance that "the road taken" was right.

Yet the Colloquium was more the gathering of a community of faith than an honor for me. It was an affirmation of the convictions that bind us together. I am deeply grateful for the privilege of being a part of a community that shares a common catholic, protestant, and reformed faith, a common way of life, and a common hope for life.

1. Some of John H. Leith's former students had sponsored "A Colloquium in Honor of John Haddon Leith: Ministry in the Life of the Reformed Church Today," at Union Theological Seminary in April of 1989.

I am grateful that we share the common conviction that the church lives not by human virtues, wisdom, or techniques, but by God's grace, by hearing God's word, and by the ministries of preaching, teaching, and pastoral care.

Remembering is, I know, a sign of age, but remembering with gratitude is a human and a Christian virtue.[2] Czeslaw Milosz in his Nobel lecture declared that the tragedy of our time is "the refusal to remember."[3]

Christmas is properly a remembering of the grace of God in the birth of a savior and of human graces that may be the means of God's grace.

John H. Leith

---

2. Phil 1:3.

3. Milosz, *Nobel Lecture*, 14.

# 18

# Christmas 1990

CHRISTMAS GREETINGS are profound in their significance. Enduring human relations are sustained by a shared loyalty that transcends who we are and what we share on the horizontal level. This shared loyalty makes it possible to survive as friends amid the changing conditions of life.

Those who receive this greeting share three common commitments. (1) "We believe in order to understand" (Augustine); (2) "Faith seeks understanding (intelligibility)" (Anselm); (3) Jesus Christ is the Word made flesh, God in his self-expression embodied in a human life.

Jesus Christ, the Word made flesh, is not a meaningful symbol or a manner of speaking. For Christians, he is the truth, an event in our history.

The secular, pluralistic influences of our society, especially in the elite media and the secular universities, have undermined the Christian confession and witness.

Yet there are hopeful signs.

During the past century, Communism, with its beguiling rhetoric, using such words as justice, equality, peace, and community to influence people, was the chief alternative to Christian faith. Many Christians, especially in leadership positions, were beguiled.

During the next few decades, the chief alternative to Christian faith will likely be Islam. In the Rushdie crisis, the Islamic community in England made clear they would not fit in a "liberal" society. The "liberal" society has given virtual "sacred" quality to status as a racial, ethnic, cultural, or national *minority*. The Islamic community in Britain insisted it did not want to be accepted on the basis of race, ethnic origin, or culture. It asked for acceptance on the basis of a community of faith that believes its faith is true.[1]

Communism may be understood as God's judgment on the moral lethargy of the Christian community. Islam is judgment on the anemic faith of Christians who in a secular, pluralistic context forget the faith is true. The Word *did* in actual fact become flesh.

There are good signs this Christmas: (1) thriving local congregations and (2) clear affirmation of transcendence, as in "Can We Be Good Without God?" by Glenn Tinder.[2] A few days ago, I heard Owen Gingerich, Senior Astronomer at the Smithsonian Observatory and Professor of Astronomy and the History of Science at Harvard, ask how people such as Carl Sagan know that this world is all there has ever been, all there is or will ever be. They have never been outside this world. For himself, Owen Gingerich, reviewing the wonder of the universe, acknowledges disclosures of the transcendent who reveals himself in the prophets and above all in Jesus Christ. The Creator is the God and Father of our Lord Jesus Christ. For this reason, Christmas is a great joy!

May we all share the joy of Christmas and rejoice in the possibilities of a New Year.

John H. Leith

1. Weller, "The Rushdie Controversy in Inter-Faith Relations," 39.

2. Tinder, "Can We Be Good Without God?" 69–85.

# 19

# Christmas 1991

M Y HOPE for you is the Joy that Christmas brings: Joy in creation, Joy in being alive, and the Joy of salvation through Jesus Christ.

A few weeks ago I read "The Gospel For This World" by Robert L. Calhoun, the most brilliant teacher I ever knew. The following sentences speak to us in a time when so few can acknowledge the facts of church life, and so many are victims of self-deception and illusion:

> Two great moral principles . . . appear again and again in Jesus' teaching and practice:
>
> The first is a demand for intelligence and integrity: not simply shrewdness nor technical competence nor rule-of-thumb honesty (though all these have their places) but a fundamental readiness in all situations to see and acknowledge what is so. The temptation stories, the Sermon on the Mount, the sayings that deal with cup and platter, unwhitened graves, ceremonial cleanliness, the Sabbath day, all reflect, in one way or another, Jesus' insistence on truthfulness and realism in the presence of an objective order that men disregard at their peril. It should not be necessary at this late day to insist that the moral and religious teaching of Jesus is not that of a light-

hearted visionary but that of one who insists at every step that realities shall be squarely faced. Intellectual and moral integrity, clear eyes and candid minds, are required of all who seek to follow his lead. In a time like ours, it seems not too much to say, these things are prime necessities not merely for would-be Christians but for all men who have to share in the job of cleaning up wreckage and rebuilding a badly damaged world. One cannot work hopefully at that task without recognition of inexorable order—natural and moral order—maintained by the power of God.

An equally essential factor in this moral summons is the demand that men live by faith, hope, and love toward God and their fellows. More concretely, this is a call for unstinting generosity in thought and action, for readiness to give more than one expects to get, for refusal to see either God or man solely within the bounds of legal stringency. This is not a contradiction of either the realistic temper or the recognition of moral order. As regards every fellow man it is a well-warranted insistence that the complexity and incompleteness of his behavior at any particular moment be given full weight in our dealings with him. As regards oneself it is a reminder that callous or cruel action reacts promptly upon one's own character, and that generosity and forgiveness do likewise, so that in very truth life is measured to us with the measures we ourselves use. As regards God the demand extracts from us recognition that if he is inexorably just, his very justice is creative and gracious. He who is sovereign is Father, in whose utmost rigor there can be promise of new gifts.[1]

1. Calhoun, "Gospel for This World," 33–34.

At Christmas personal friendships are renewed by the Communion of Saints in which we participate, and the common faith and hope that we share. I hope for you a joyous Christmas and the best New Year ever.

John H. Leith

## 20

# Christmas 1992

A T CHRISTMAS we know the joy of creation and the joy of redemption, for the Creator is the Redeemer.

So you and I who share so much—Union Theological Seminary, the Presbyterian Church, the vocation to proclaim the gospel—rejoice in the human joys of friendship, the vitalities and energies of life and all the good things of this life as well as God's redemption of the world in Jesus Christ, the means of grace and the hope of glory.

God's grace is the origin of creation and redemption.

> We cannot avoid saying that Jesus Christ's Incarnation is an analogue of creation. Once more God acts as the Creator, but not now as the Creator out of nothing; rather God enters the field and creates within creation a new beginning, a new beginning in history and moreover in the history of Israel.[1]

May this be a very merry Christmas for you and the best New Year ever.

John H. Leith

1. Barth, *Dogmatics in Outline*, 97. See Christmas 1999 below.

# 21

# Christmas 1993

I CAN remember at least seventy Christmases. My earliest memories include my mother hanging a picture of Jesus and a picture of Santa Claus in our home, decorating the Christmas tree and hanging the stockings, and the Christmas play at the church.

There has never been a year without Christmas or, for that matter, without a Christmas tree except for the years I was a graduate student in New Haven.

In good years and bad, Christmas has always meant wonder, awe, joy and human happiness. Singing the Christmas carols has without exception been a powerful means of grace. (Can we not limit "Advent" to one Sunday? I doubt if three members of my seminary class had ever heard the word in 1943.)

I am glad, as many of you have heard me say, that the Santa Claus festivity as well as the tree, the log, the lights, the Christmas gifts and cards were added to the remembrance of Christ's birth. They have certainly been a means of human grace and also of divine grace. They are the joy of creation, sacraments of its goodness.

Christmas is a joyous moment when there is so much bad news in the public order and worldwide and when the news in the organizational life of the church and many of its institutions is so dismal.

I think that Christmas this year will be a wonderful break from the front pages of the newspapers and the affairs of the organized church. It will bring a new awareness of the wonder of human life, of loved ones and of friends. Above all, Christmas celebrates the love of God who became flesh and dwelt among us, full of grace and truth. Apart from this there would be no joy in creation and no hope for our broken lives. And no Santa Claus.

I hope this Christmas the grace of God in Jesus Christ will bless each one of us. I am confident that when Christmas is over we shall with new confidence and power preach and teach the gospel in a Reformed way in the places in which in the providence of God we do our work.

May you have the most blessed New Year ever.

John H. Leith

## 22

# Christmas 1994

CHRISTMAS 1994 is like Christmas 1993: for me nostal-gia for Christmases past, the joy of Christmas present and the theological hope, if not political, economic, cultural or ecclesiastical hope, for the future.

The Christmases of my childhood are today, sixty to seventy-two or seventy-three years later, a source of great strength, proving that the practices of faith are equal to or are of greater importance than the study of theology for the Christian life. A Marine, whom I know, may have forgotten many things he had learned, but he found strength and bless-ing in preparing a Christmas tree in the Vietnam jungle.[1]

Some of you have expressed amazement, if not dis-approval, that last year I wrote that the memory of more than seventy years of my mother hanging a picture of Santa Claus along with the picture of Jesus in our home was a great blessing to me. You had a point but only if my asser-tion was not theologically qualified.

I still affirm my thanks for my mother's hanging the pictures, which incidentally I found recently in her things, and I affirm my belief in Santa Claus at the age of seventy-

---

1. This refers to John H. Leith's son, Henry W. Leith, who served his nation as a Marine and who is now a carpenter in Goochland, Virginia.

five. I also affirm my thanks for the joy of creation so evident at Christmas. Yet these assertions must be theologically qualified.

When we confess our faith, we have to pray, "Lord, I believe, help my unbelief."[2] But at Christmas the important fact is the confession.

Hanging a picture of Jesus and a picture of Santa Claus or believing in Santa Claus or enjoying the many joys of creation at Christmas is safe and constructive only if with all our hearts we believe and intend to believe that Jesus Christ is the embodiment of God in human life and that God raised Jesus from the dead. If we believe the ancient Nicene Confession, then we are free to enter into all the joys of creation. If we do not believe and confess the Nicene faith, the joys will turn to dust and ashes in our hands, and life will come to a meaningless end.

This question of the Nicene faith is *the* crucial question facing the Presbyterian Church, its structures as well as its seminaries, its ministers of the word and all its members especially at Christmas.

Some theologians, e.g., Pannenberg, and some social scientists, e.g., Wuthnow, have raised questions whether the mainline churches shall survive into the twenty-first century. They have also indicated that all the evidence points to the survival of the "evangelicals." I would add many Presbyterian congregations show all signs of surviving into the 21st century and beyond.

Apart from the Nicene Confession, why should anybody bother with the church, that is, apart from belief in a personal God who acts personally in history and creation,

2. See Mark 9:24.

Jesus Christ who is God embodied in a human life, the resurrection of Jesus Christ, eternal life. Apart from this confession there are many organizations in our society more useful than the church. If the church is not the community of the Nicene faith, why bother with it?

The new knowledge society, according to a recent article by Peter Drucker, has replaced the old communities—village and congregation and family—with voluntary organizations.[3] The organization is not a community but a tool, a means to an end, a technology. This is why the church also has to have in our time an organization as a means to certain ends. But the church, as Luther and the entire Protestant Reformation reminded us, is not an organization.

This Christmas I believe that the church, as a community of faith and life, constituted by hearing the gospel of God's grace in Jesus Christ, is possible in this secular society. It will support people in living with dignity and serenity amid the crises and challenges of human existence and also enable them to grow in the image of Jesus Christ.

The celebration of the birth of the Messiah is crucial in our society. It is worth noting that the origin of the Nicene Creed was contemporaneous with the designation of December 25 for the celebration of the birth of Jesus. This choice of December 25 deliberately set the celebration of the birth of Jesus over against the nature gods that were so popular then and are again so popular in our society. As Augustine knew in the fourth century, we worship not the sun but the Son who created the sun.[4]

My own hope for this Christmas is that from about December 15 I shall spend much time listening to the old

3. Drucker, "Age of Social Transformation," 53–80.
4. See Christmas 2000 below.

Christmas carols and reading the birth narratives. The simple Christmas carols and the birth narratives state what we believe really happened at the birth of Jesus better than much, if not all, sophisticated theology.

How can we say more clearly what *really* happened on the first Christmas than what is said in the story of the shepherds to whom the angels appeared? Ironically, if some churches, captivated by Advent, a novelty in our Presbyterian tradition, forget the carols, we can be grateful that the secular malls will teach them to the children.

But we can be sure that in our own lives and in the church, we shall be blessed, renewed, and strengthened at Christmas by the singing of carols, by reading the birth narratives. We can go into 1995 with the human poise, dignity and serenity that can be given only by faith in the God and Father of our Lord Jesus Christ.

John H. Leith

*I am increasingly made happy by the life and work of students who took seriously what I have attempted to teach. My way of being a pastor and a Christian theologian was and is certainly not the only way. Only God knows the true value of anything. And all of our work we have to commit to Him with a prayer for forgiveness. Yet this Christmas, on the human level I am very proud of the life and work of my friends. Thank you.*

# 23

## Christmas 1995

A HEART attack concentrates the mind, as they say, but it can be a means of grace, both of divine grace and human grace. I hope that each of you knows how much the greetings by mail and telephone meant. The heart attack made me more aware that I belong to a great human community and a great community of Christian faith in the Reformed and Presbyterian way.

I hope this Christmas letter will convey the same personal meaning to you. I am grateful first of all at this season for the Christmas joy that a Savior has been born but next to that and because of that I am grateful for the human joy of friendship and comradeship in a common faith.

I have no new words for this Christmas letter. I still believe, as I have indicated in previous letters, in Santa Claus, Christmas cards, Christmas gifts, Christmas parties, and family celebrations.

I hope to finish my Christmas duties early so that I can spend much time, as Christmas approaches, listening to the old familiar Christmas carols that have always been, and in old age are more so, a means of God's grace.

Christmas declares that the Word, God in God's self-expression, became flesh, embodied in a human life, full of grace and truth.

We must declare this Word in a secular society that either rejects it or relativizes it. We must proclaim it in its fullness in the church and bear witness to it in the civic clubs and in academic theology, and even in seminaries and church colleges where it is sometimes relativized or denied.

Richard Hocking once told me that his father, W. E. Hocking, a very distinguished professor of philosophy at Harvard University, was so overwhelmed by the sheer wonder of Luke's Christmas story that he would break down in tears when he read it to his family on Christmas day. We must recover this sense of wonder and awe that the Word became flesh.

Christmas in a remarkable way unites the personal and the material. God who is the true Person, became embodied in a human life, in a body of flesh and blood. Hence I do not take too seriously all the rhetoric about the commercialization of Christmas. I increasingly think it is a wonderful thing that at Christmas we enjoy God's creation. We like to eat good food; we like to share gifts, and have joyous reunions with friends. Let us this Christmas use the material as a means to enhance and keep human life human. Let us offer our prayers and thanksgiving to the Creator who gave to us not only our persons but our bodies and this wonderful world in which we live.

In recent years I have become increasingly aware of the fragility and transitoriness not only of human life but also of human institutions, even those we cherish the most.

For many human beings life is cut off before they achieve its fullness, and institutions that we cherish and that have taken centuries to build can be lost in a very brief time.

The joy of Christmas that the angels announced to the shepherds is not fragile but is the same today, tomorrow and forever. This gives us hope amid the fragility and transitoriness of our life and of the human communities and institutions that we cherish.

I am grateful for what friends mean to me, to the church and to the human community. I wish for you a very joyful Christmas and the best New Year ever.

John H. Leith

# 24

# Christmas 1996

I CAME to know only recently the Christmas carol "In the Bleak Midwinter." It did not at first appeal to me, but as I heard it sung, it became increasingly meaningful to me.

> In the bleak midwinter,
> Frosty wind made moan,
> Earth stood hard as iron,
> Water like a stone;
> Snow had fallen, snow on snow,
> Snow on snow,
> In the bleak midwinter,
> Long ago.[1]

This carol honestly acknowledges reality, the stubborn facts of the world of nature as well as the world of history. This sense of reality is a precondition for hearing the good news of the birth of Jesus. Open acknowledgment of reality is closely related to that which the New Testament and theology call repentance. What happened at Christmas becomes more wonderful in this context than it ever can amid the tinsel, neon lights, and the mad rush of Christmas shoppers.

---

1. Rossetti, "In the Bleak Midwinter," stanza 1. See Christmas 2000 below.

In 1960 I read Erich Auerbach's *Mimesis*, and I have never forgotten his emphasis upon the style of the biblical narratives: their great sense of objective reality, an emphasis upon the concrete, an awareness of the significance of human actions in the context of the physical world as well as the social, an emphasis upon decisions, responsibility, integrity. This biblical quality comes to focus in the birth narratives of Matthew and Luke.

Mary and Joseph are not nobility but truly human people whom we can recognize and who immediately have credibility with us. They live amid the concrete realities of physical and historical existence, making decisions that everyday people in every time and place have had to make.

Later artists would attempt to change the style of the narratives. The stable becomes a palace. Mary and Joseph become nobility. The realism of the birth narratives returns with the concrete, realistic style of Rembrandt.[2]

Raymond Brown, the distinguished Roman Catholic New Testament scholar, has written that the story of the shepherds is the distinctively Protestant narrative. You cannot do very much to cover up the ordinary, rural, concrete reality of the shepherds. The wise men on the other hand were subject to style change. They became nobles, the wealthy, the elite with fancy gifts.

It is clear from previous Christmas letters that I delight in the joys of Christmas: the Christmas trees, the lights, the exchanging of gifts and greetings, the festivals of Christmas. These are the joys of creation. Yet they are possible only because created existence without any decoration was appropriate for the Word to become flesh, to be embodied in a truly

2. See Christmas 1974 above.

human life that could have been and was mistaken by many as only an ordinary human life. The real joy of Christmas is the good news that God the Father almighty, maker of heaven and earth, is the Father of our Lord Jesus Christ.

The Christmases I knew as a boy were very concrete and very real. Maybe the Depression, more than faith, made them so. The ornaments, the meals, the celebration were simple. In my family we had oyster stew on Christmas Eve when my uncle and aunt were our guests. Christmas was very plain and the decorations were few and simple. The conversation was the unadorned speech of ordinary people. Yet there was something very awesome about the evening. Perhaps for this reason I have always tried to have oyster stew on every subsequent Christmas Eve, though the context has changed, not necessarily for the better.

The concrete realism of the birth narratives has much to teach us. Our society, even in the church, has learned how to cover up reality and live in a make-believe world. We have lost the capacity to take responsibility for our own lives, to be who we are. We have to recover authenticity and responsibility, in particular, the wisdom and power to discriminate among values and options, to declare publicly what we believe, to take a stand in the presence of opposition.

I like people who respond to indicative sentences with indicative sentences. I like to talk to people whose words authentically convey the feelings of their hearts and the thoughts of their minds. Yet I increasingly talk to people who have erected a wall around themselves. What they say is what they want you to hear, not what they really think or feel.

I hope this Christmas enables us to recover personal authenticity in what we say and also a renewed capacity

to perceive reality, the physical and social reality that sur-
rounds us, and to make our own critical judgments without
being blown about by every wind of doctrine and every
career ambition.

I shall read the birth narratives a number of times before Christmas with these thoughts in mind. I hope also to
spend much time listening to tapes of Christmas carols that
I have collected. Increasingly they convey to me the gospel
and the truth about what happened in the birth of Jesus.

I hope for you the joy of Christmas and the best New
Year ever.

John H. Leith

# 25

# Christmas 1997

CHRISTMAS HELPS give me my identity, perhaps even more, if among friends I can border on heresy, than Baptism but less than the father and mother who conceived me in a particular family, church and society, and less than the election of God, if I may recover my orthodoxy.

You have heard me say the simple, but awe-filled Christmases that I knew even through my college years are among my best memories and shaped my life. More people return to the church at Christmas than any other time. I can understand that.

I hope that this Christmas will be a time when you and I renew and strengthen our identity as Christian people. I intend to read the Christmas stories and John 1:1–14, to listen to Christmas hymns, and to an English rendition of Bach's "St. John Passion." I hope this Christmas I will have more free time for what is most important.

My comments thus far have been stimulated by an article in *First Things* that I found profound[1] and also by the casual use of first names that I abhor. The use of first names in the context of friendship and respect is very meaningful. But the use of first names outside the context of friend-

---

1. Kass and Kass, "What's Your Name?" 14–25.

ship is presumptive and even rude. First names preserve anonymity or over-emphasize the individual. This is the crucial point: the first name does not tell us who we are. The last name identifies the family and tradition to which we belong.

The first or given name is bestowed in Baptism in the name of the Father, Son and Holy Spirit. The last name places us in a family, a history, a tradition and a culture. Last names, surnames, are very recent in our culture. They became common in Europe and Britain only in the sixteenth century, though they were required in China by an edict of the emperor in 2852 BC.

Names may be no more than signs designating a thing or an individual. They can be substantive, telling the world who we are.

Our name is not the only source of our identity. The celebration of Christmas powerfully shaped my understanding of who I think I am. The simplicity, the awe-filled days leading up to Christmas, the reading of the narratives, the singing of the carols in the context of family and church told me who I was.

Christmas is only one source of our identity. The church got along without Christmas for more than three centuries. The Puritans outlawed it. But Christmas has persisted. In our secular society it is the pre-eminent public festival. Let us make the most of it for our Christian edification. Let us tell the secular society why there is a Christmas just as we must tell them boldly why there is a millennium. In addition, the only ground for the joy we experience at Christmas is what God did in Jesus Christ for our salvation.

Otherwise, the joy of Christmas is a cruel joke, as Bertrand Russell knew.

Christians under the leadership of a monk, Dionysius Exiguus, began in the sixth century to measure time from the birth of Jesus, not from the founding of Rome. The Christian community believed the most important date in world history was Jesus Christ who embodied in a human life the Word of God. Christians live not in the year of Rome or any other human event, but in the time when God became incarnate and wrought our salvation.

When the Edinburgh Presbytery of the Church of Scotland adopted as its celebration of the millennium the issue of homelessness under the banner "Room at the Inn, AD 2000," my friend David Wright protested with words we should ponder:

> The most worrying feature of this widespread tendency to seize on incidentals and to magnify them out of all proportion is this: it so often reflects a loss of confidence in distinctively Christian essentials. So Christmas becomes a baby-festival or family reunion, or a binge of good-will to all and sundry (for which the Authorized Version translation of Luke 2:14 is partly to blame!), or even a campaign against homelessness rather than a celebration of the incarnation of God's Son 'for us men and for our salvation.' . . . The psychology of this shift is easily understood. As the central truths of the Christian faith attract less and less allegiance in the community, so churches and ministers endeavor to retain a place in the sun by diverting their energies into activities which unbelievers will applaud and support.

These are often wholly commendable causes; measures to tackle homelessness are always good. But the good may become the enemy of the best, if less and less of the church's expenditure of time, effort and resources . . . [do not pass] this simple test: is it doing or saying what no-one else but the Christian church will say or do? The less the life of the church satisfies that decisive criterion, the more it will approximate to a purely humanitarian agency. And then who will explain to an ignorant and perhaps questioning world where on earth or in heaven the date AD 2000 comes from?[2]

"Go, tell it on the mountain, over the hills and everywhere; go, tell it on the mountain that Jesus Christ is born!" Thereby we shall establish our identity in a culture dominated by the secularism of the elite media and modern university and also by the paganism as well as the secularism of much of television. "Go, tell it on the mountain that Jesus Christ is born."

May each one who reads this letter know the joy of Christian faith and have the best New Year ever.

John H. Leith

---

2. Wright, correspondence.

## FAVORITE HYMNS OF JOHN HADDON LEITH

*John DeBevoise and Palm Ceia Presbyterian Church gave me a wonderful gift—a tape of the hymns, Psalms and carols I cherish.*

### Hymns

"How Firm a Foundation"
"If Thou But Suffer God to Guide Thee"
"Now Thank We All Our God"
"A Mighty Fortress Is Our God"
"Come, Thou Fount of Every Blessing"
"All Creatures of Our God and King"
"When I Survey the Wondrous Cross"
"Beneath the Cross of Jesus"
"Amazing Grace"
"Thine Is the Glory"
"God of Grace and God of Glory"
"O Beautiful for Spacious Skies"
"For All the Saints"
"God of Our Fathers"
"Love Divine, All Loves Excelling"
"Just As I Am"
"God Is Working His Purpose Out"
"Onward, Christian Soldiers"

### Psalms

"All People That on Earth Do Dwell"
"The Lord's My Shepherd"
"The King of Love My Shepherd Is"
"O God, Our Help in Ages Past"
"O Lord, Our Lord, in All the Earth"

## Christmas Carols

"Come, Thou Long-expected Jesus"
"While Shepherds Watched Their Flocks by Night"
"It Came Upon the Midnight Clear"
"What Child Is This?"
"Hark, the Herald Angels Sing"
"O Little Town of Bethlehem"
"O Come, All Ye Faithful"
"Joy to the World!"
"Silent Night! Holy Night!"
"In the Bleak Midwinter"
"Go, Tell It on the Mountain"

# 26

# Christmas 1998

CHRISTMAS HAS come and also the darkness of the winter solstice. Yet Christmas is the same, a light shining in the darkness. Our human situation changes, though I remember Christmases of seventy-five years ago in continuity with Christmas today. We are now residents of the Presbyterian Home of South Carolina, a wonderful facility but a difficult and even traumatic change in life.

Christmas this year will be the most meaningful ever, though there are no "stockings or toys," but an abundance of Christmas symbols and decorations throughout the home.

First, Christmas is joy in the created world. The world of flesh and blood is good because God, the Almighty Father, created it. This world is good also because it is not all there is. Christmas brings us a greater joy than creation. Hence human reunions, good food, greetings and Christmas cards, gifts, the sheer joy of being alive do not end in nothingness but are part of God's eternal kingdom.

Second, the gospel makes possible not only the forgiveness of sins but provides also the foundation of our joy. Without the death of Jesus for our sins and without God raising Jesus, the crucified and risen Lord, from the dead no real joy could bless our lives. Good Friday and Easter give substance to Christmas.

Third, Christmas is the answer to the hopelessness that oppresses our world from Russia, to Post Second World War Europe, to Britain and the hopeless notes written for Diana, and now to the United States. Apart from Christian faith there is no answer to the problem of death and the end of history. A European philosopher recently concluded that man is a recent invention. He will soon disappear as a face drawn in the sand. Therefore let us sing vigorously, "Joy to the World!"

Fourth, we read a lot about the 21$^{st}$ century and the third millennium. Yet we can be sure the elite media and the modern universities, the most secular communities in our society, and the evangelistically timid bureaucracies of the Presbyterian Church and the ecumenical organizations will not tell the world why there is a millennium. If the world is to know the significance of BC and AD, on the millennium, Christian ministers who believe with passion that Jesus Christ is God incarnate, Savior and Lord, will have to preach boldly. It is a joy to me that most who receive this greeting will surely do that.

John H. Leith

> *Caroline[1] found an old tape of a sermon I preached in*
> *1990, which she played on the car radio as she drove*
> *us to Bob Brearley's installation at St. Simons Island.*
> *The sermon said what I still believe. It was delivered*
> *ad lib and typed from the tape. For this reason it may*
> *be more authentic. You are under no obligation to*
> *read it unless you want to read it.*

## WHEN THE ANGELS WENT AWAY, WHAT THEN?

Let us pray: Almighty God, creator of heaven and of earth, thou whose thoughts are beyond our imagining, we thank thee that thou hast placed thy word nigh unto us in Jesus Christ our Lord. Grant that this day Jesus Christ may speak to us by his word and by his Spirit, as our prophet to teach us how to live and how to die, as our priest to make amends for the evil that we do, as our king to rule over us and to defend us from all evil. Give us hearts that are open to the prompting of thy Spirit. Through Jesus Christ our Lord. Amen.

### Scripture: Luke 2:1–16

Last Sunday we gathered here in anticipation of Christmas, last Tuesday we celebrated Christmas, and this is now the Sunday after Christmas, and on Tuesday we shall take down the lights and throw out the Christmas tree. And more significantly, during these days we have sung the great

---

1. This refers to John H. Leith's daughter, Caroline H. Leith, elder at Grace Covenant Presbyterian Church, Richmond, Virginia, and a member of the board of directors of the Foundation for Reformed Theology.

Christmas carols, and our hearts have known the joy of the faith that the Creator has come to us in Jesus Christ. And perhaps we have known the ecstasy of this faith. But now, as in the stories of the birth, the angels went away, and the question is, "What shall we do now?"

Some year ago, Ogden Nash published a poem, "A Carol for Children," which strikes a chord that all of us in certain moments have known. It goes like this:

> God rest you, merry Innocents,
> Let nothing you dismay,
> Let nothing wound an eager heart
> Upon this Christmas day. . . .
>
> Soon, soon enough come crueler gifts,
> The anger and the tears;
> Between you now there sparsely drifts
> A handful yet of years. . . .
>
> Two ultimate laws alone we know,
> The ledger and the sword—
> So far away, so long ago,
> We lost the infant Lord.
>
> Only children clasp his hand;
> His voice speaks low to them,
> And still for them the shining band
> Wings over Bethlehem.
>
> God rest you, merry Innocents,
> While innocence endures. . . .[2]

2. Ogden Nash, "A Carol for Children," 218. See Christmas 1980 above and Christmas 1999 below.

Well, you and I are no longer innocent, and we have known the joy of singing that he reigns in truth, in nature, and in history, but we read in the papers of the threatened war in the Middle East, the clash of economies and of societies in disarray. We are no longer innocent. We have heard the carols, which tell us in very vivid ways what Christians believe happened in Jesus Christ, but the question on the Sunday after Christmas is, "What does this mean in our everyday life?"

We have sung "O little town of Bethlehem, How Still We See Thee Lie; Above thy deep and dreamless sleep The silent stars go by. Yet in thy dark street shineth The everlasting light. The hopes and fears of all the years Are met in thee tonight."[3] But the secularity of our culture, of our centers of information, such as the great universities and especially the mass media, the events which we read about in Bethlehem itself make it very difficult for us to affirm that "the hopes and fears of all the years are met in" a street in Bethlehem.

And in addition to the question of faith, we're all tired. And like Elijah of old, who in the morning took on Jezebel and all of her hosts but when he became weary, fled, and his faith was not restored until his physical energies had been replenished, so today in the face of the perils of the Sunday after Christmas, what shall we do?

Let us first of all reaffirm the miracle of Christmas, the faith of the carols that we have sung, and then let us ask quite specifically, "What do we do when the angels go away?"

---

3. Brooks, "O Little Town," first stanza.

The New Testament is a miraculous book, miraculous in the sense that it is everywhere predicated upon the
conviction that there is a transcendence, an intelligence, a
purpose, a higher love, beyond this world which we can see
and taste and touch and handle, and that this transcendent
love and purpose invades our history and the nature of the
world in which we are a part and in particular has become
embodied in the life of a human being, Jesus Christ. This
is a great miracle. We hear on television that this world
that we see is all there is, all there has ever been, all there
ever will be. But I was impressed a few months ago when
I heard an astronomer who has become my friend, Owen
Gingerich, say, "How does Carl Sagan know? He has never
been outside the world."

It is our faith that there is something more, and this
transcendent purpose has been embodied in a human life.
The New Testament concentrates on the death and resurrection of Jesus Christ, which it thinks of as miracles, that
is, as acts of God. Now it's not obvious that the death of Jesus
Christ is a miracle. We know enough about deaths. People
die, and people are killed continually in our experience. But
the New Testament saw in the death of Jesus Christ not another human death but a miracle, an act of God. Here there
was actualized in human history what is always happening
in the heart of God, God taking upon himself the sin of the
world, forgiving our sins without saying it doesn't matter,
and overcoming and using the death of Jesus to triumph
over evil and sin in our world.

The resurrection of Jesus Christ is quite obviously for
our culture a miracle. The only question for our culture is,
"Did it happen?" But the witness of Christian faith and the

conviction of the New Testament is that this Christ, who was crucified, appeared as the crucified but risen Christ, and the disciples using the language of ordinary experience to describe that which is beyond ordinary experience have witnessed that they saw him, heard him, and were commissioned by him to go forth into all the world to preach, and to teach, and to baptize.

From the very beginning, the Christian church always observed the miracle of Easter. Every Sunday is an Easter, for on the first day of the week, God raised Jesus Christ from the dead. The New Testament does not concentrate upon the birth of Jesus, and the early church did not celebrate the birth of Jesus. December the 25th was observed as the celebration of the birth of Jesus no earlier than 325 in Rome and certainly by 336.

Somewhat earlier, Christians in Egypt had celebrated at times the baptism, and at other times the appearance of the wise men, and still at other time the birth of Jesus on January the 6th, the day after the waters of the Nile were supposed to have miraculous power. And in the newspaper this morning it is reported that January the 6th will be restored in Russia as a national holiday, the observance of the birth of Jesus. In Rome, too, they deliberately set the celebration of Christmas on the day when the pagan world exulted in the vitalities and energies of nature, in particular the vitality and the energy of the sun.

On the Festival of the Sun, the early Christians said, we shall observe the birth of the Son of Righteousness. We worship not the energies and the forces of the sun. We worship him who created the sun. And therefore the sun itself, with all of its vitalities and energies, is simply another part of the created world. There is in our time a revival of paganism, particularly in Europe in a more formal way. In an informal way, you would have to say that a great deal of our music, or at least it seems to me, is a return not only to paganism but to barbarism. Now, paganism is essentially the exultation of the forces of nature and the conviction that the meaning of life is to be found in the intensification of the vitalities and energies of nature. And in our society we have done very well in turning Christmas once again not into a festival of the Son of Righteousness but into a Festival of the Sun, an occasion when we can rejoice in the vitalities and energies of nature.

Now Christians ought to rejoice in the vitalities and energies of nature. They ought to enjoy eating a good Christmas dinner, for example. But we can rejoice in that because it is our conviction that the God who made the sun, the God who created human life with all of its vitalities, energies, impulses, and instincts, the God who created human flesh and blood as well as the God who created the mountains, the mystery of the ocean, the vitality of running streams, the fertility of the soil, this God is the God who confronts us in Jesus Christ.

And so the early church said, "In the beginning was the Word"—the mind of God, God in God's self-expression—"In the beginning was the Word, and the Word was with God, and the Word was God, and all things were made through him, and without him was not anything made that was made. . . . And the Word became flesh"—embodied in a human life—"and dwelt among us, full of grace and truth."[4] This is the real truth about the world. You cannot find the

4. John 1:1–3, 14.

real truth about the world in biology books, or history books, or astronomy books, or chemistry books. The real and final truth about the world is Jesus Christ. And that's what the early Christians said. The Jews had looked for a Messiah, but they thought this was not the right Messiah. But the Greeks had also been moved by the quest for truth: What is nature? What is Truth? And for centuries they had, as no other people in the history of the human race ever has, puzzled with the question, "What is truth?" And here Christian people, simple people, came to those who were heirs of this great philosophic tradition and said, "If you really want to know what the truth is, we have the answer in Jesus of Nazareth."

That is the miracle of Christmas. And that is the miracle we proclaim over against, and in the midst of, a highly secular culture. Let me say, this does not mean that Americans are secular today. There is overwhelming evidence that Americans are more religious today than they have ever been. But the centers of information, which control information in our society, are secular and are secularizing, in particular, the universities and the mass media.

In May 1954, *Time Magazine* took a poll of twenty-eight prominent Americans, including a prominent editor of a Richmond newspaper—they did not reveal how he voted—but they asked these twenty-eight prominent Americans to list the 100 most important events in human history. And the event that they listed as number one was Columbus's discovery of America. That was before the National Council of Churches had informed them that they should not celebrate that event as a good thing in the history of the human race. And the second most important event was Gutenberg's discovery of moveable type. The crucifixion of Jesus was tied for fourteenth place.

Now, one may argue on the basis of verifiable consequences that Jesus Christ created greater changes in human history than any other one event, but that conclusion is debatable. But if Jesus Christ is who Christian people believe he is, the embodiment of the wisdom and power of God the creator, then this is the most important event that has ever happened, the most important event that can ever happen, and the greatest responsibility you and I have is to be witnesses to what took place in Bethlehem in the year AD 1. And that is the reason we in the Christian church say, "Before Christ" and "In the year of our Lord," for Jesus Christ is the dividing point of time.

Well, we have affirmed the miracle, and later we shall sing, "Silent Night! Holy Night!" We have already sung "Joy to the World!" But we cannot celebrate Christmas all the time. We cannot be continually singing carols. We have to ask, when the angels go away, "What shall we do?" And each of us must answer that question for himself or for herself.

But let me suggest two commitments, or if someone wants to put it differently, two New Year's resolutions, that will reaffirm this faith, shape our lives for the better, and contribute a great deal to our life in this church and in society. And the first is, we can resolve, we can commit ourselves, to read the Bible through this year. Now, if someone doesn't quite make it, that may be very well. I'm not exactly sure that I shall read Numbers and Leviticus. But there are few things we can do that would be more useful than committing ourselves this year to read through the Christian Scriptures. Even Alan Bloom, a Jew, declares that the Christian Scriptures are by far the most influential book in the shaping of American life. It is only in a culture that took the Bible seriously, not only for religious faith but for the commonwealth, that political democracy in its truest and real form emerged. It is the language of our faith, and it deepens faith. If half of this congregation would resolve to read the Bible through this year, if one-fourth of the congregation would resolve to do it, human lives would be transformed, this congregation would be deepened in its spiritual commitments, and life in Richmond would be better.

And we can determine in the second place that one year from now we shall be more mature Christian human beings than we are today. To use an old phrase, we can resolve that this year we shall give attention to our sanctification. In Sunday school this morning we sang the hymn, "Take Time to Be Holy." We can take this year as a time to be holy.

Now what does it mean to be sanctified, and what does it mean to be holy? Well, let me suggest that to be sanctified, to be holy, means that we come to trust God as our Father in heaven, that we accept life as his gracious gift and live in gratitude and humility, that we have an openness to our neighbor, a humaneness to our disposition. To be sanctified means that we have an increasing capacity to detach ourselves from things. To be sanctified means that we have an increasing awareness that we are obligated, that we are responsible, that we are answerable for the time and the energy that has been entrusted to our keeping and what we do with it. This is what it means to be holy: trust in God, gratitude and humility, humaneness and openness, the capacity to detach oneself from things, to commit one's life to God's care, the sense of being accountable, answerable, obligated, the desire to contribute more to the world than one takes out of the world.

And then, we have to ask the question, I think, in this congregation in another sense. When the angels went away, what shall we do? The most pressing task for this congregation, it if is to go in haste as the shepherds did, to see the birth of the Christ child, the most pressing task of this congregation is to proceed in haste to appoint a committee to get a minister and to proceed in haste to call and persuade an effective minister to come here as pastor of this church. Anyone who looks at the quantifiable data of this congregation is aware that the future of this congregation is very precarious and problematic unless a dedicated, competent, and effective minister is called and persuaded to come here. It is almost axiomatic that anyone who wants to come cannot do the job. In the past twenty-five years no one, I think, in the Presbyterian Church has had more opportunity to observe pulpit committees, similar to this one, in operation than I have. And on the basis of that experience, I can say that churches and pulpit committees generally get the kind of minister they deserve.

There has been in our church a decline, it seems to me undeniably, in the theological maturity, and in the competence, of pulpit committees. And this decline in the competence of pulpit committees is intimately related to the decline in the Presbyterian Church. And moreover, the task of calling a minister, an ancient procedure and doctrine in the church, has been replaced by the secularized personnel policies of American business, and it's quite obvious they haven't worked too well in American business in the last twenty years. And moreover, there have been procedures enacted that both protect mediocrity and enhance mediocrity.

The great task of a pulpit committee is to go out and find someone and persuade that person to come in. I shall never forget the advice given to me by David Mullins, who was once the distinguished President of the University of Arkansas, but when I knew him, he was Dean of Faculty at Auburn, where I was pastor of a church. "The Bear Bryants," he said, "do not interview or apply for the job." Hence, the most important and pressing task, when the angels have gone away, is for this church to call into existence a committee that can do the job and for them to go out and find and call and persuade a person to come here who can build this church up in membership and in the communion of saints.

And having celebrated Christmas we ought to know that the first and most decisive qualification for any member of the pulpit committee is the passionate conviction that Jesus Christ is the word made flesh, that God in Jesus Christ brought our salvation, and that God raised Jesus Christ from the dead. No one ought to be on any pulpit committee without that passionate faith! And by the same token, the only minister who can revive the fortunes of this congregation as a community of faith is one who is passionately convinced that Christmas is true, that Jesus Christ is Emmanuel, God with us, and that God raised Jesus Christ from the dead.

Well, we've sung the Christmas carols, and now the angels have gone away, and the great challenge of the faith is to live this year so that the faith of the Christmas carol and of the Christmas story will shape and fashion our lives, and when we gather here next Christmas we shall have read the Bible through and we shall be more holy and more sanctified than we are now. Amen.[5]

5. John H. Leith, "The Miracle of Christmas."

# 27

# Christmas 1999

O GDEN NASH declared that Christmas is for children, at least as long as they are innocent of the hard realities of the world.[1]

Children do enjoy Christmas oblivious of the harsh realities of the world. Yet so do we as old people. We lay aside our worries and fears and participate in the joys of creation: food and drink, Christmas greetings and cards, Christmas trees, Christmas lights and family dinners. As old people we do rejoice with some of the innocence of childhood.

Yet Christmas is for old people because we *have* experienced the crueler gifts of which Nash spoke. Old people know that the two great challenges are *death* and the *end of history*. The issues with which we spend so much time are secondary: race, environment, social justice, the feminist movement, sexuality and homosexuality are all secondary.

The secular elite media and the secular university, like communism, have no answer to the challenge of death. Unfortunately the bureaucratic church and many theologians in colleges and seminaries give a very muted response. In fact one seminary professor made Christmas obsolete,

1. Nash, "A Carol for Children," 218. See Christmas 1980 and Christmas 1998, "After the Angels Went Away, What Then?" above.

declared that Jesus is not necessary for faith, presumably because his faith does not include a personal God who became incarnate and who raised Jesus from the dead.

Yet in many local congregations the answer is bold and clear in song, in Scripture, in many sermons, and in the response of the people. At Christmas believers boldly declare that the origin of all things is a personal God who is personally active in creation and history, who became incarnate in Jesus, the Word made flesh, who when wicked men crucified him, God raised him from the dead, who then appeared to his disciples who recognized him and heard him as the crucified but risen Jesus as he commissioned them to go into all the world to preach, teach and baptize.

Christmas is a *miracle*, not just another human event. In a magnificent chapter on the mystery and miracle of Christmas, Karl Barth wrote:

> Once more God acts as the Creator, but now not as the Creator out of nothing; rather, God enters the field and creates within creation a new beginning. . . . In the continuity of human history a point becomes visible at which God Himself hastens to the creature's aid and becomes one with him.[2]

In song and in many sermons this faith is proclaimed at Christmas and by this proclamation the church lives.

As an old man (eighty years) I have seen three generations come and go. I know the temptation to say that life is without meaning, and the end of all things is the debris of a universe in ruins.

2. Barth, *Dogmatics in Outline*, 97. See Christmas 1992 above.

Christmas is a great joy to old people as to children. Let us this Christmas boldly declare the miracle of Christmas in a secular world that does not believe Christmas faith is possible and in the church over against the Jesus Seminar, the theologians and the preachers who have muted the faith or given it up, whose work destroys local congregations and denominations. My great hope for the Christian community is today found in the vibrant faith of many local congregations.

Let us this Christmas celebrate Christmas out of the joy of our hearts and also as our witness to the world.

I hope for all those within the reach of this Christmas greeting a faith filled Christmas and the best New Year ever. I also want to thank those who have helped me along the way, for the reality of the communion of saints, especially those who have studied with me and shared with me a common ministry of the Word, made flesh, and raised from the dead.

John H. Leith

# 28

# Christmas 2000

EASTER COMES in the spring when the days are growing longer and the weather more pleasant. Light and warmth have overcome darkness and the cold. Moreover, flowers are sprouting; some are even blooming and the grass is growing.

Christmas comes at the winter solstice when the days are short, dark and cold. Darkness and the cold are partly alleviated for us by electricity and new heating systems. We can remember, if we are old enough, how dark and cold it was at the winter solstice a century or less ago.

> In the bleak midwinter,
> Frosty wind made moan,
> Earth stood hard as iron,
> Water like a stone;
> Snow had fallen, snow on snow,
> Snow on snow,
> In the bleak midwinter,
> Long ago.[1]

We, who live in the Northern Hemisphere, can understand why Christmas plays a much larger role with us than

1. Rossetti, "In the Bleak Midwinter," stanza one. See Christmas 1996 above.

in does in the New Testament and in the early church. We understand why the yule log, the Christmas greenery and the lights, as well as gifts and Santa Claus, play so large of role in our celebration of the birth of Jesus.

Last Christmas I wrote that the really great question facing human beings is death and the end of history. I know this on a personal level now even better than a year ago.[2] The problem of guilt does not arise until we have some word to speak over against death and the end of history, over against the fragileness and certain doom, not only of human persons but also of institutions and communities, over against the terrible aloneness in a world without a God who knows us by name.

Christmas means that God is personal and personally active in the created order of nature and history. Augustine said, "We worship not the sun, but the Son of righteousness who created the sun."[3] Christmas means that the God who created the world has become embodied, in so far as God can become embodied, in a human life in Jesus of Nazareth. We therefore call him the Son of God. God did personally enter our condition, was crucified and buried. The climax of our faith is the affirmation that Jesus of Nazareth was raised from the dead by God. The lives of the disciples were transformed and the Christian church (congregation) was established when they became witnesses of the crucified and risen Lord, who commissioned them to go forth in all the world and proclaim this gospel of a God who is active in human history and who is more powerful than death.

2. John H. Leith's wife, Ann White Leith, had died on March 8, 2000.
3. See Christmas 1994 above.

I do not know exactly what to make of the story of the shepherds as a historian, but as a theologian, I cannot think of a better way of saying what Christians believed happened in the birth and life, death and resurrection of Jesus Christ.

> While shepherds watched their flocks by night,
> All seated on the ground,
> The angel of the Lord came down,
> And glory shone around.
>
> "Fear not," said he—for mighty dread
> Had seized their troubled mind—
> "Glad tiding of great joy I bring
> To you and all mankind.
>
> "To you, in David's town this day,
> Is born of David's line
> The Saviour, who is Christ the Lord!"[4]

It is worth observing that Christmas began to be celebrated shortly after the church affirmed the full deity of Jesus Christ as the Council of Nicaea. Only a passionate faith and a joyous conviction that Jesus is the Word (the mind of God) made flesh enables us to truly celebrate Christmas in a secular culture.

Today I am very proud that so many ministers, who studied with me, as preachers proclaim in a secular society the ancient truth that the Word did become flesh and dwells among us full of grace and truth. This is our song and our proclamation this Christmas for our salvation, and for the salvation of those who will hear.

I wish for each of you the joy of Christmas and the best New Year ever.

John H. Leith

4. Nahum Tate, "While Shepherds Watched Their Flocks," stanza 1, 2, and part of 3.

# 29

# Christmas 2001

SOME MONTHS ago, when I was unable to go to church, I heard Jerry Falwell preach a sermon entitled "The Fourth Quarter."[1] As I am in the fourth quarter or in overtime, it caught my attention.

Football games always have four quarters, but human life does not necessarily have a fourth quarter, or even a third quarter, much less an overtime. The fourth quarter in human life comes by the grace of God, and it offers some of the same opportunities that a fourth quarter does in football or basketball.

Life in the fourth quarter, as in a football game, is determined by what has happened in the first, second and third quarters. The first, second and third quarters greatly limit what can done in the fourth quarter. On the other hand, the first, second and third quarters can make the fourth quarter a time of real achievement. A good strategy in life, as in a football game, is to prepare in the early quarters for the fourth.

Football games are complete at the end of the fourth quarter or overtime. Human life is never complete in history. Every person, like Moses, dies looking into the promised land. No matter how much we have achieved we always

1. Falwell, "Fourth Quarter."

can imagine ourselves having achieved more. We cannot exhaust the possibilities of life and therefore, the fourth quarter of human life always ends in a certain sense of frustration. Human life can only be completed by God. The promise of the resurrection of Jesus Christ and eternal life saves human life from ending in meaningless emptiness and the joy of young and old at Christmas from being an illusion. All of this sounds like a preparation for Easter rather than for Christmas; yet, I am evermore convinced that Christmas is for old people as well as children. Perhaps especially for old people. Solzhenitsyn, at eighty-three, has written, "Aging thus is in no sense a punishment from on high, but brings its own blessings and a warmth of colors all its own."[2]

Christmas represents the coming of God into our human life. "The Word became flesh and dwelt among us."[3] Insofar as God can be embodied in a human life, God was embodied in Jesus Christ. Jesus Christ is the final word of God not in the sense that God no longer reveals Himself but that every revelation of God is to be judged by the revelation of God in Jesus Christ.

Christmas means that the created world is good. In the birth of Jesus creation became the habitation of the Creator Himself. Let us rejoice and be glad in it. Joy and human exuberance is as much a part of the Christian life as soberness and sorrow. At Christmas time we greet each other in a friendly way; we send Christmas cards; we give gifts to those who are near and dear to us; we are compassionate and help those who are in need. All this is the wonder of Christmas.

Christmas Eve has always been an awesome time for me, especially as I remember my experiences as a boy. Now

2. Solzhenitsyn, "Growing Old," 322.
3. John 1:14.

in old age we experience the awesomeness of what happened in the birth as well as the mystery and wonder of human existence itself.

I rejoice in the Christmas carols, which always have been for me a very powerful means of grace. I hope this Christmas to enjoy them as never before and I hope you do.

I have said in recent letters that the great theological question that all of us must face and answer is death and the end of history. If we cannot find the gospel in death and the end of history, then we have very little to say to human beings on this planet.

I have always been interested in the fact that people are eager to argue about the beginning of the world, but do not argue about how the world ends, though that is the more serious problem for all of us. Christmas, I think, contributes a great deal to our understanding of the meaning of death and the end of human history. We have the security of knowing that the God who made the world is the God who gives life. He is the God who sustains His creation and will see it through to the end.

Many of your have heard me say that I would never send out a Christmas card unless I could address it. I take that back this year, as my hands are in such a situation that I cannot address many letters. I shall, however, sign my name.

I thank God for all the students I have taught and for the magnificent ministries that so many have accomplished and for their witness to the Gospel we know at Christmas as well as at Easter.

Have a merry and blessed Christmas and the best New Year ever!

John H. Leith

# Bibliography

Auerbach, Erich. *Mimesis: The Representation of Reality in Western Literature.* Translated by Willard R. Trask. Garden City, NJ: Doubleday, 1957.

Augustine. *City of God.* In Nicene and Post-Nicene Fathers, edited by Philip Schaff. First Series, volume 2, 1–511, translated by Marcus Dods. Peabody, MA.: Hendrickson, 1995.

Bach, Johann Sebastian. "St. John Passion."

Baillie, John. *The Sense of the Presence of God.* The Gifford Lectures, University of Edinburgh 1961–62. New York: Scribner, 1962.

Barth, Karl. *Church Dogmatics.* Edited by G. W. Bromiley and T. F. Torrance. Four volumes, in twelve parts, plus index. Edinburgh: T. & T. Clark, 1936–77. Cited by volume, part, and page. Study Edition, in thirty-one paperback fascicles. London and New York: T. & T. Clark, 2009.

———. *Dogmatics in Outline.* With a new Foreword by the author. Translated by G. T. Thompson. New York: Harper, 1959.

Bloom, Allan [David]. *The Closing of the American Mind: How Higher Education Has Failed Democracy and Impoverished the Souls of Today's Students.* New York: Simon and Schuster, 1987.

Brooks, Phillips. "O Little Town of Bethlehem," 1868. *The Hymnbook*, 157, hymn 171. Richmond, VA: Presbyterian Church in the United States, 1955.

Butterfield, Herbert. *Herbert Butterfield: Writings on Christianity and History.* Edited with an Introduction by C. T. McIntire. New York: Oxford University Press, 1979.

Calhoun, Robert L. "The Gospel for This World." In *Making the Gospel Effective*, edited by William K. Anderson, 25–34. Nashville: Commission on Ministerial Training, Methodist Church, 1945.

Calvin, John. *Commentary on the Epistles of Paul the Apostle to the Corinthians*, volume 1. Translated from the original Latin and collated with the author's French version by John Pringle. Grand Rapids: Eerdmans, 1948.

Ciardi, John. "In Place of a Curse." In *39 Poems*, 13. New Brunswick, NJ: Rutgers University Press, 1959.

Cuddihy, John Murray. *No Offense: Civil Religion and Protestant Taste.* New York: Seabury, 1978.

Drucker, Peter F. "The Age of Social Transformation." *Atlantic Monthly* 274 (November 1994) 53–80.

Eccles, John C. *The Human Mystery.* The Gifford Lectures, University of Edinburgh 1977–78. Berlin, Heidelberg, New York: Springer International, 1979.

Eccles, John C., and Daniel N. Robinson, *The Wonder of Being Human: Our Brain and Our Mind.* New York: Free Press, 1984.

Falwell, Jerry. "Fourth Quarter Ministry." On line: http://trbc.org /new/sermons.php?url=20010805.html

Hook, Sidney. *Out of Step: An Unquiet Life in the 20th Century.* New York: Harper and Row, 1987.

Jaki, Stanley L. *Angels, Apes, and Men.* La Salle, IL: Sherwood Sugden, 1983.

Johnson, Paul. *Modern Times: The World from the Twenties to the Eighties.* New York: Harper and Row, 1983.

Kass, Amy A., and Leon R. Kass. "What's Your Name?" *First Things* 57 (November 1995) 14–25.

Kilpatrick, James J. *The Writer's Art.* Kansas City: Andrews, McMeel & Parker, 1984.

Leith, John H. "The Miracle of Christmas." Audiotape of sermon also referred to as "When the Angels Went Away, What Then?" Richmond, Virginia: Grace Covenant Presbyterian Church, December 30, 1990.

Luccock, Halford E. "Christmas Day in the Morning." In *The Christian Century* 65 (December 22, 1948) 1392.

Luther, Martin. "Ninety-five Theses." Translated by C. M. Jacobs and revised by Harold J. Grimm. In *Career of the Reformer*, volume one. Luther's Works 31 Philadelphia: Muhlenberg, 1957.

Milosz, Czeslaw. *Nobel Lecture.* New York: Farrar Straus Giroux, 1980.

Nash, Ogden. "A Carol for Children." In *Many Long Years Ago*, 218. New York: Little, Brown and Company, 1938.

Niebuhr, H. Richard. *The Responsible Self: An Essay in Christian Moral Philosophy*. With an Introduction by James M. Gustafson. New York: Harper & Row, 1963.

Niebuhr, Reinhold. *Leaves from the Notebook of a Tamed Cynic*. Reprint, New York: Da Capo, 1976.

Outler, Albert C. *The Rule of Grace*. Melbourne: Uniting Church of Australia Press, 1982.

———. "The World So Loved by God." In *The Preacher: Sermons on Several Occasions*, edited by Bob W. Parrott, 223–31. Nashville: Abingdon, 1988.

Peters, Thomas, and Robert H. Waterman Jr. *In Search of Excellence: Lessons from America's Best Run Companies*. New York: Harper Collins, 1983.

Rossetti, Christina. "In the Bleak Midwinter," c. 1872. *The Presbyterian Hymnal*, 36. Louisville: Westminster John Knox, 1990.

Solzhenitsyn, Aleksandr Isayevich. "Growing Old." In Joseph Pearce, *Solzhenitsyn: A Soul in Exile*, 322–23. Grand Rapids: Baker, 2001.

———. "Nobel Lecture." In *The Solzhenitsyn Reader: New and Essential Writings 1947–2005*, edited by Edward E. Ericson Jr. and Daniel J. Mahoney, 512–26. Wilmington, Del.: ISI Books, 2006.

Tate, Nahum. "While Shepherds Watched Their Flocks," 1700. *The Hymnbook*, 155, hymn 169. Richmond, VA: Presbyterian Church in the United States, 1955.

Temple, William. *The Church Looks Forward*. New York: Macmillan, 1944.

———. *Religious Experience, and Other Essays and Addresses*. Collected and edited with an introduction by A. E. Baker. London: J. Clarke, 1958.

Tinder, Glenn. "Can We Be Good Without God?" *Atlantic Monthly* 264 (December 1989) 69–85.

Turner, James. *Without God, Without Creed: The Origins of Unbelief in America*. Baltimore: Johns Hopkins University Press, 1985.

Visser 't Hooft, Willem A. *Rembrandt and the Gospel*. NBC-TV, Frontiers of Faith, 1960. The National Council of the Churches of Christ in the U.S.A., Broadcasting and Film Commission. The Library of Union Theological Seminary in Virginia. 1994.

Weller, Paul. "The Rushdie Controversy in Inter-Faith Relations." In Dan Cohn-Sherbok, editor, *The Salman Rushdie Controversy in Interreligious Perspective*, 37–57. Symposium Series 27. Lewiston, N.Y.: Edwin Mellen, 1990.

Wright, David F. Correspondence.